Bible Study

52-Week KJV Bible for Women

Denise Gilmore

© 2021 by ADISAN Publishing AB, Sweden

No part of this publication may be reproduced, stored in a retrieval system, or transmitted in any form or by any means, electronic, mechanical, photocopying, recording, scanning, or otherwise as permitted under section 107 and 108 of the 1976 United States Copyright Act, without the prior permission of the Publisher.

All scripture quotations, unless otherwise stated, are taken from The Authorized (King James) Version. Rights in the Authorized Version in the United Kingdom are vested in the Crown. Reproduced by permission of the Crown's patentee, Cambridge University Press

Limit of Liability/ Disclaimer of Warranty: The publisher and the author make no representations or warranties concerning the accuracy or completeness of this work's content and expressly. Neither the Publisher nor the author shall be liable for damages arising here.

Table of Contents

•

Introduction

Many women may be wondering how to start reading the Bible. They may also be doubting how they could get through the Bible in a year. They might even be curious about how the Bible relates to their lives and what they are going through. Who will they read the Bible and study it with? Who can they start small groups with? How do they go through the Bible in a year?

We hope that the 52-week KJV Study Bible will help women of all ages do just that: sit down and read God's word together as a group. We hope that this Study Bible will help more and more women come together to better understand who God is, what His mercies are, and what they mean for them in their everyday lives. God longs for women everywhere to know Him on a deep and personal level.

This easy-to-read KJV Study Bible is aimed to help women understand how to approach the Bible from beginning to end. From the book of Genesis to the book of Revelation, there are so many inspiring stories that women can relate to and learn from. They can learn about the first recorded sin that led to the fall of the entire world in Genesis, to the bravery of Esther when she saved her people from Haman's evil plot, all the way to the second coming of Jesus in the book of Revelation.

Women will learn how to overcome struggles with confidence and to find out more about themselves and their own character with each lesson. This 52-week KJV Study Bible will help women everywhere have a week-by-week opportunity to dig deeper into God's word over a year. This study Bible will also allow more and more women to discover the incredible truths about God, His mercies, and His love for them.

We hope that this study Bible inspires many women to take the time to sit down together and really enjoy reaping the benefits as well as taking in the knowledge that comes with reading God's word together every week.

How to Read This Book

This KJV Study Bible can be started at any time of the year, at week 1. With each week, women will go from book to book of the Bible. Each lesson starts out with reading scripture. It explains the scripture, followed by discussion questions that women can discuss as a group. Then at the bottom of each lesson, they will see personal journal questions to ask themselves individually.

This study Bible can even be used as an individual study Bible for those women who want to dive deeper into God's word by themselves. Having no set date for the study Bible weeks helps women decide when to start reading it.

It has easy-to-read explanations and discussion questions that each woman can discuss alone or with a group. The journal questions at the end of each lesson allow each woman to look back and think about the beautiful things they have learned not only about God but to think about the fantastic things they've learned about themselves each week.

We hope that this KJV Study Bible helps women learn more about God and apply what they have learned to their lives with every week's lesson.

WEEK 1

SCRIPTURE READINGS:

Day One: Genesis 3:1-2 (Temptation)

Day Two: Genesis 3:4-7 (Satan's Lie)

Day Three: 1 Corinthians 6:9-10 (Entering God's Kingdom)

Day Four: 1 John 1:6 (Cleansed from Unrighteousness)

Day Five: Ephesians 5:11-12 (Rebuke Unfruitful Works)

Day Six: Romans 3:20 (Knowledge of Sin)

Day Seven: Mark 7:20 (Guard Your Mouth)

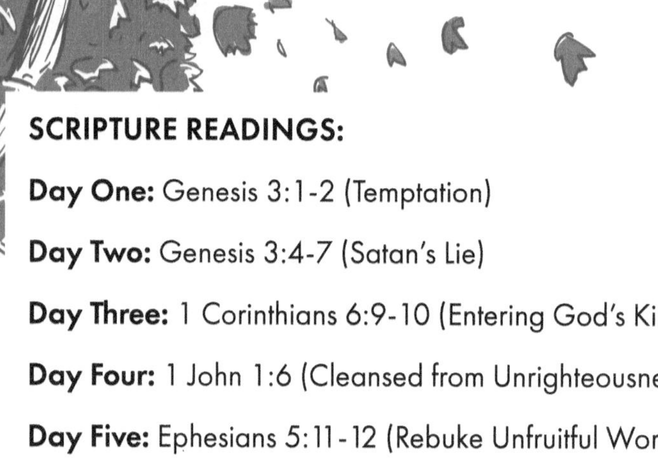

"⁴ And the serpent said unto the woman, Ye shall not surely die:⁵ For God doth know that in the day ye eat thereof, then your eyes shall be opened, and ye shall be as gods, knowing good and evil.⁶ And when the woman saw that the tree was good for food, and that it was pleasant to the eyes, and a tree to be desired to make one wise, she took of the fruit thereof, and did eat, and gave also unto her husband with her; and he did eat.⁷ And the eyes of them both were opened, and they knew that they were naked; and they sewed fig leaves together, and made themselves aprons." Genesis 3:4-7

Eve was the first woman of the Bible. She was deceived by Satan to eat from the Tree of Knowledge of Good and Evil in the middle of the Garden of Eden. God had told her to not eat or touch that specific tree in the Garden of Eden; otherwise, she would die. But Satan tricked her into thinking it would make her wise like God and help her know the difference between good and evil. She felt the tree looked pleasing and that the food was good to eat, so she tried it. Not only did she eat from the tree, but she also convinced Adam to eat food from the tree. Eve was the first person to sin in the Bible. The Garden of Eden was a lush paradise for both Eve and Adam. Now, thanks to Eve and her mistake, every woman on earth is subjected to sin and temptation every day.

After she and Adam had eaten the fruit from the tree, their eyes were opened to the fact that they were naked. They both had never realized that they were naked until after they sinned. They were trying to cover up the sin they'd just committed by sewing aprons together to hide their nakedness. Before they'd sinned, they lived in harmony with God, and they weren't ashamed of their nakedness. However, after they sinned, they became ashamed because they had disobeyed God.

Whenever you are confused about what God may be saying to you, remember Satan's lies can come in many forms. In this instance, he took the very words from God and twisted God's words to make them look different. Satan then told Eve that she wouldn't die if she ate from or touched the Tree of Knowledge of Good and Evil. Satan can make anything, and everything that God tells you seem different than what He has really said to you. Eve believed what Satan had told her instead of obeying the direct order that she had received from God to not eat from or touch the Tree of Knowledge of Good and Evil. It can be tempting to not listen to God because, at certain times, God's commandments seem like they're too hard to follow. If you're told not to do something, Satan makes you feel like it's ok to do it anyways. What can it hurt? As you can see, the first sin led to the fall of all mankind. It can be effortless to fall into Satan's twisted web of lies and deception.

DISCUSSION QUESTIONS:

Have you ever been tricked by Satan to do something that you shouldn't do? How did Satan make it seem you weren't really sinning?

____

____

____

____

____

After you sinned, were your eyes opened the way Eve's eyes were opened? Did you realize more about yourself than before you had sinned?

____

____

____

____

____

Did you ask for forgiveness or try to cover your sin up like Eve and Adam did?

____

____

____

____

How did you come before God and ask forgiveness from your sin?

____

____

____

____

JOURNAL QUESTIONS:

What sins have you committed against God?

____

____

____

____

____

Did they ever seem like they weren't such a big deal? What did you learn from them?

____

____

____

____

____

How can you resist Satan's attacks? How can you stop yourself from sinning?

____

____

____

____

____

The Blame Game Starts

SCRIPTURE READINGS:

Day One: Genesis 3:12 (Adam Blames Eve)

Day Two: Psalm 119:33 (The Lord's Decrees)

Day Three: Proverbs 10:19 (Hold Your Tongue)

Day Four: 1 Peter 4:8 (Love Deeply)

Day Five: Luke 6:45 (Store Good in Your Heart)

Day Six: James 3:10 (Don't Curse)

Day Seven: Romans 8:8 (Realm of The Flesh)

¹⁰ "And he said, I heard thy voice in the garden, and I was afraid, because I was naked; and I hid myself. ¹¹ And he said, Who told thee that thou wast naked? Hast thou eaten of the tree, whereof I commanded thee that thou shouldest not eat?¹² And the man said, The woman whom thou gavest to be with me, she gave me of the tree, and I did eat.¹³ And the Lord God said unto the woman, What is this that thou hast done? And the woman said, The serpent beguiled me, and I did eat."
Genesis 3:10-13

After Adam and Eve had committed the first sin, they were very aware that they were naked. They were also ashamed and afraid of God and tried to hide from Him. When God asked where they were, Adam admitted that he and Eve were hiding from Him because they were afraid. God asked them if they'd eaten from the Tree of Knowledge of Good and Evil, and Adam cast the very first case of the blame on Eve. He told God the woman He had given to him to keep him the company had convinced him to eat from that tree, and he ate from it. God then asked Eve what she had done. In turn, she cast the second case of the blame on the serpent, saying she had been tricked by him.

Let this passage be a lesson for you. Casting blame on someone else for something that you did is never the right thing to do. When you cast blame, you're trying to shift the focus off of you to make someone else look guilty. When Eve cast the blame on Satan, she tried to take the focus off of herself and say to God, "Satan messed with me and deceived me. He made me think it was not a big deal if I disobeyed you, Lord. Satan made me think it was ok to eat from the Tree of Knowledge of Good and Evil. It's his fault, not mine." She was trying to focus and the guilt off of herself and make Satan look like an entirely guilty person.

Even though it was Satan's fault for deceiving Eve, it was also Eve's fault for acting on Satan's deception instead of listening to God. It was also Eve's fault for tricking Adam and saying that it was ok for him to eat from the tree. Both Eve and Satan made it seem as if the first sin was no big deal. What Eve didn't realize was that she committed the first sin, and because of that mistake, she had separated not only herself and Adam from God, but she separated the rest of the world from God from that point on.

She should've realized that the commandment to stay away from the Tree of Knowledge of Good and Evil came directly from God. She didn't know that Satan was corrupt and would deceive her. Thanks to Eve, every woman can learn which voice is God's and which voice is Satan's. Every woman can also learn that if someone tells you something that seems too good to be true, it probably is too good to be true.

DISCUSSION QUESTIONS:

Have you ever blamed someone for deceiving you and tempting you to do something you shouldn't, instead of openly admitting that you sinned?

Is there hostility between you and another person because of sin?

How do you repair the relationship with that person and with God?

JOURNAL QUESTIONS:

Have you ever been afraid that someone would find out about a mistake you've made?

Have you ever blamed someone for a mistake that you made?

How do you approach God, asking His forgiveness for your sins?

WEEK 3

Cursed with Hard Labor

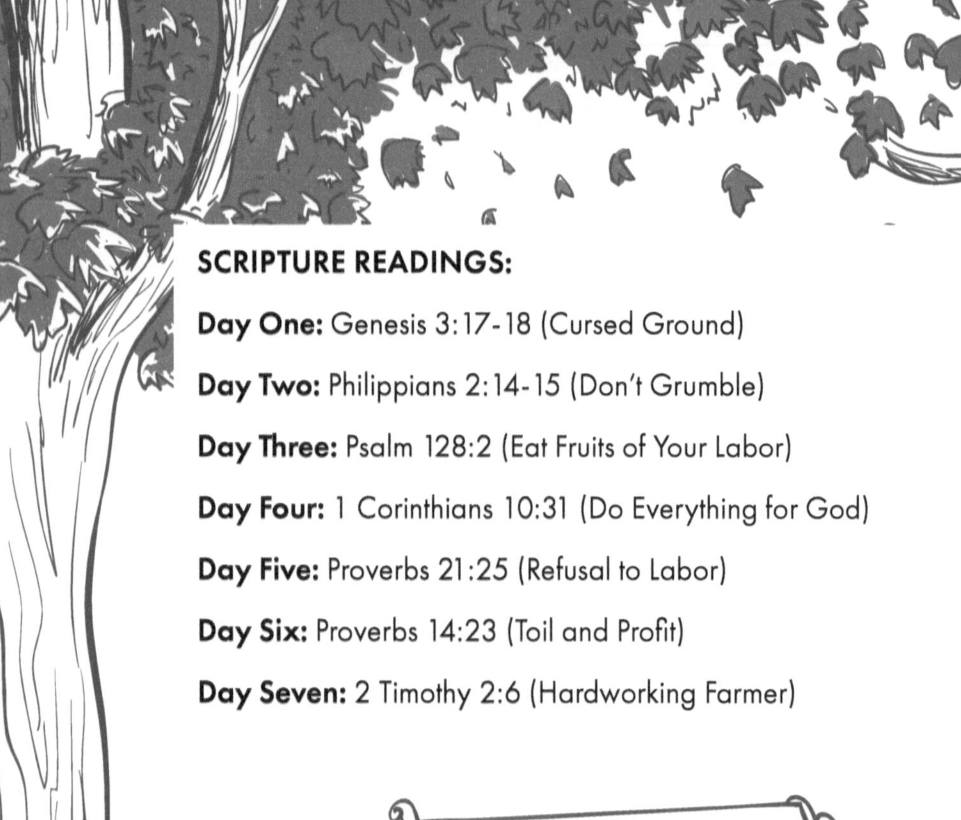

SCRIPTURE READINGS:

Day One: Genesis 3:17-18 (Cursed Ground)

Day Two: Philippians 2:14-15 (Don't Grumble)

Day Three: Psalm 128:2 (Eat Fruits of Your Labor)

Day Four: 1 Corinthians 10:31 (Do Everything for God)

Day Five: Proverbs 21:25 (Refusal to Labor)

Day Six: Proverbs 14:23 (Toil and Profit)

Day Seven: 2 Timothy 2:6 (Hardworking Farmer)

"¹⁷And unto Adam he said, Because thou hast hearkened unto the voice of thy wife, and hast eaten of the tree, of which I commanded thee, saying, Thou shalt not eat of it: cursed is the ground for thy sake; in sorrow shalt thou eat of it all the days of thy life;¹⁸ Thorns also and thistles shall it bring forth to thee; and thou shalt eat the herb of the field;... ²⁰ And Adam called his wife's name Eve; because she was the mother of all living.²¹ Unto Adam also and to his wife did the Lord God make coats of skins, and clothed them." Genesis 3:17- 18,20-21

All because Adam had listened to his wife Eve instead of listening to God's direct order, God cursed the ground that Adam would work every day. God then told Adam that the ground he would work to bring food for his family would be cursed because he had been deceived and tempted by his wife Eve and had eaten from the Tree of Knowledge of Good and Evil. Thorns and thistles and hard labor would be in the way of Adam getting food every day. With much sweat, blood, pain, and tears, Adam had to work to provide for his family. Instead of everything being comfortable and them being able to eat and drink whatever they wanted at any time they pleased, in paradise and in harmony with God, Adam and Eve had to work very hard to get food and water and provide for their family.

That's a very severe punishment for the first sin. Now, every person on Earth has to work extremely hard to make a living. Everyone goes through temptation, sin, and hard times every day of their lives. Think about how hard you've had to work to provide for your family and make an honest living. With much hard work, you labor every day to provide for your family, cook, clean your house, and to keep a roof over yours and your family's head every day.

The name for Eve came because she was then known as the mother of all living things. The fantastic thing is that God still showed love to Adam and Eve even after they sinned against Him. He even made coats of animal skins for them and clothed them so they wouldn't be cold.

God dealt Adam and Eve such a severe punishment for the first sin because He wanted to get His point across about what to expect if someone disobeyed Him. If Eve hadn't sinned or caused Adam to sin, the world wouldn't be full of trials, turmoil, or pain.

Everyone would live in harmony with one another. We would also be more loving towards one another and obey God willingly every day of our lives. Since the first sin, everyone has had trials and temptation follow them every day of their life. You will have trials and temptation as a woman too. Satan's temptation comes in many different forms, so always be on your guard so you can resist him. Guard your heart, mind, body, and soul diligently against Satan's lies and deception. Cling to God's truth.

Had it ever occurred to you that you're working as hard as you are, mainly because of the first sin?

____

____

____

____

____

Do you wonder what a perfect world would've been like?

____

____

____

____

____

Do you think the punishment for sin was too severe or just severe enough?

____

____

____

____

____

JOURNAL QUESTIONS:

How do you go about your life even though you struggle with temptation and sin every day?

Do you ever think of the first sin and how that has affected your life? How are you tempted by Satan every day?

What things can you do to resist him?

WEEK 4

SCRIPTURE READINGS:

Day One: Genesis 12:13-17 (Abram's Plan)

Day Two: Proverbs 10:9 (Crooked Person Revealed)

Day Three: Proverbs 12:22 (Abomination to God)

Day Four: Psalm 52:2 (The Tongue Plots Destruction)

Day Five: Galatians 6:7-8 (Reaping and Sowing)

Day Six: Galatians 5:16-17 (Desires of The Flesh)

Day Seven: James 1:22 (Doers of The Word)

¹³ "Say, I pray thee, thou art my sister: that it may be well with me for thy sake; and my soul shall live because of thee.¹⁴ And it came to pass, that, when Abram was come into Egypt, the Egyptians beheld the woman that she was very fair.¹⁵ The princess also of Pharaoh saw her, and commended her before Pharaoh: and the woman was taken into Pharaoh's house.¹⁶ And he entreated Abram well for her sake: and he had sheep, and oxen, and he asses, and menservants, and maidservants, and she asses, and camels.¹⁷ And the Lord plagued Pharaoh and his house with great plagues because of Sarai Abram's wife." Genesis 12: 13-17

Sarai was going to Egypt with Abram, and when they got close to Egypt, Abram said that he knew Sarai was a beautiful woman for men to look upon. He came up with a plan to deceive Pharaoh and tell him that Sarai was his sister instead of his wife. Abram and Sarai lied to Pharaoh and the other Egyptians, so Abram wouldn't get killed. They both knew that if Pharaoh knew that Sarai was Abram's wife that Abram would be killed. The Egyptians saw how beautiful Abram's wife Sarai was. Even Pharaoh's daughter, the princess, saw how beautiful she was and took Sarai to stand before Pharaoh himself.

At that time, Pharaoh had not known that both Abram and Sarai were lying to him about who Sarai really was. He didn't realize that Sarai was really Abram's wife. Because he didn't know, he treated Sarai very well for Abram's sake. Abram was given sheep, cattle's and donkeys. Pharaoh even blessed Abram with menservants, maidservants, and female donkeys and camels. Abram was living his best life because of the deception that he had created. But then God sent plagues upon Pharaoh and his household because of Sarai and Abram's deception.

Let this passage teach you a lesson not to lie to anyone, period. Let it also teach you not to lie to anyone who is a higher authority figure in your life, whether your parents, grandparents and extended family member, a supervisor, or your boss at work. Do not lie, just to protect yourself or someone else from physical, emotional, or mental harm. Do not lie to anyone because God knows that you're lying even before you think about lying in the first place. He even knows the reason you will lie before it's even in your mind to lie. He already knows that you will lie to protect your reputation before you even act on the lie. He knew that Abram and Sarai would lie to Pharaoh for their own good. That's why He sent plagues upon Pharaoh and his household to tell him that there was something wrong.

The next time you're tempted to lie about your relationship with your husband or boyfriend, to your family or your friends or your coworkers, remember the punishment that Abram and Sarai got because they chose to lie to Pharaoh. A lie is a lie, no matter how big or small. If you lie to anyone, remember, God already knows, and it'll only be a matter of time before someone else discovers the truth.

Have you or your husband ever been tempted to lie to your friends, family, or coworkers to cover up your relationship?

____

____

____

____

____

Have you or your husband ever lied to someone to save face or lied to keep you both safe?

____

____

____

____

____

Did anyone ever find out about the lie?

____

____

____

____

____

Have you ever lied to anyone about your relationship with your husband?

Were you afraid of your family's or friend's reaction to your relationship?

How did God help you have the courage, to tell the truth?

WEEK 5

SCRIPTURE READINGS:

Day One: Genesis 16:2-5 (Sarai Gives Hagar To Abram)

Day Two: Hebrews 13:14 (Marriage Shall Be Honored)

Day Three: Proverbs 6:32 (Lacking Sense)

Day Four: Mathew 5:27-28 (Committing Adultery)

Day Five: Exodus 20:14 (Do Not Commit Adultery)

Day Six: 1 Corinthians 6:18 (Sin Inside the Body)

Day Seven: Deuteronomy 22:22 (Laying in Sin)

[2] "And Sarai said unto Abram, Behold now, the Lord hath restrained me from bearing: I pray thee, go in unto my maid; it may be that I may obtain children by her. And Abram hearkened to the voice of Sarai. [3] And Sarai Abram's wife took Hagar her maid the Egyptian, after Abram had dwelt ten years in the land of Canaan, and gave her to her husband Abram to be his wife. [4] And he went in unto Hagar, and she conceived: and when she saw that she had conceived, her mistress was despised in her eyes. [5] And Sarai said unto Abram, My wrong be upon thee: I have given my maid into thy bosom; and when she saw that she had conceived, I was despised in her eyes: The Lord judge between me and thee." Genesis 16: 2-5

Sarai, Abram's wife, had not been able to have any children, and she felt guilty that she could not conceive children for Abram to be a father. So, she decided to give Hagar, her maidservant, to Abram to be his new wife. She let Hagar have sex with Abram so he would be able to have children. Yes, as shocking as it may seem, you read that correctly. Sarai let her husband have sex with another woman that he was not married to just so he could be a father. The even crazier part of this story is that Abram actually listened to Sarai. He went along with her plan to sleep with Hagar. He slept with Hagar, and she conceived a child.

When Sarai had seen that Hagar had actually become pregnant, she was extremely jealous of Hagar. She started to despise Hagar, and she even put the blame on Abram and told Abram that he was the one that was wrong to sleep with Hagar, even though she had given them both permissions to sleep with one another. She'd said now that Hagar knew that she would have Abram's child, Hagar started to despise Sarai. Sarai said that she hoped the Lord would judge both her and Abram for the wrongs they'd committed against each other.

Let this Bible passage be a lesson to every woman who may not be able to conceive naturally. You can learn a valuable lesson from Sarai, Abram, and Hagar. Do not come up with outlandish schemes or plans unless you're fully prepared to deal with the consequences of those decisions. Do not give your husband the idea or the permission to sleep with another woman just so he can become a father unless you are prepared to deal with the emotions and the consequences of that decision.

Do not blame your husband for going through with the idea if you're the one who gave him the idea in the first place. Every action has consequences. Instead, let this passage teach you to be grateful for the things you do have instead of complaining about the things you don't have. Do not despise someone just because they have something that you want. Do not hate a woman because she's pregnant and you're not. Instead, pray that God would bless you with a child if it is His will that you should have one.

Have you ever given your husband the crazy idea and permission to sleep with another woman because you couldn't get pregnant naturally?

____

____

____

____

____

What happened to you and your family because of that decision?

____

____

____

____

____

What lessons can you learn from this Bible passage?

____

____

____

____

____

Have you been trying to start a family? Are you having difficulty conceiving naturally?

____

____

____

____

____

Did you ever have the crazy thought of letting your husband sleep with someone else just to have a kid?

____

____

____

____

____

If that thought entered your mind, how did God stop you from potentially hurting your family and your marriage?

____

____

____

____

An Angel Appears to Hagar

SCRIPTURE READINGS:

Day One: Genesis 16:9-11 (Angel Talks to Hagar)

Day Two: Genesis 16:13 The God Who Sees)

Day Three: James 1:17 (Perfect Gifts)

Day Four: John 14:26 (The Lod's Helper)

Day Five: Revelation: 12:1 (Sign from God)

Day Six: Luke 24:44 (God's Spoken Words)

Day Seven: Deuteronomy 7:9 (Keep God's Commandments)

"⁹ And the angel of the Lord said unto her, Return to thy mistress, and submit thyself under her hands.¹⁰ And the angel of the Lord said unto her, I will multiply thy
seed exceedingly, that it shall not be numbered for multitude.¹¹ And the angel of
the Lord said unto her, Behold, thou art with child and shalt bear a son, and shalt
call his name Ishmael; because the Lord hath heard thy affliction. ¹³ And she called
the name of the Lord that spake unto her, Thou God seest me: for she said, Have
I also here looked after him that seeth me? And Hagar bare Abram a son: and
Abram called his son's name, which Hagar bare, Ishmael." Genesis 16: 9- 11, 13

Abram then told Sarai to deal with her mistress Hagar as she pleased.
Sarai started to mistreat Hagar, so Hagar fled from her. While Hagar
was in the wilderness, the angel of the Lord found her by a fountain.
He asked her where she had come from and where she was going. Hagar then
admitted that she was fleeing from Sarai because Sarai had mistreated her. After
all, she resented her. The angel of the Lord then told her to go back to Sarai and
to submit to her, which means to do whatever she was asked.

The angel of the Lord told her that He knew that she was going to have Abram's
child. He also said to her that He would increase Hagar's descendants so they
would be too many to count and for her to give the son that she was to have the
name, Ishmael. The angel also explained that the Lord had heard and seen her
misery and had taken pity on her. He then described Ishmael in detail, saying
that he would be a wild man against everyone and everyone would be against
him. Hagar was amazed and in awe that the Lord had seen her and taken pity
on her. She even called Him "the God who sees." Hagar said, "For I have now
seen the one who sees me."

Hagar then had the son and named him Ishmael as the angel of the Lord had
instructed her. This passage proves to women everywhere that even when you
think God is absent or that He doesn't see your pain or hear your cries, He is
still with you through every circumstance. Hagar called Him "the God who
sees," which is as true back then as it is today. He really is the God who sees all
and knows all. He still hears your cries, whether they are in your heart or mind.

He hears your thoughts and knows them whether you speak them out loud or
speak them in the silence of your own heart. He saw Hagar's misery, and He
sees yours too. He will attend to you just as He attended to Hagar. He will help
you in your times of difficulty. Trust in Him and wait patiently for Him to deliver you from your strife. Trust that He will do as He promises you. Trust that He
is with you even when it seems as though He is far away.

Have you ever been jealous of another woman because she had something you wanted?

____

____

____

____

____

Have you ever mistreated another woman that was your friend because you started resenting her?

____

____

____

____

____

How did God soften your heart?

____

____

____

____

____

JOURNAL QUESTIONS:

Have you ever been jealous of a woman that was pregnant when you wanted a child?

Have you ever mistreated a female friend because you resented her for be-ing pregnant?

Did you see God heal that woman's pain? How did God soften your heart towards the other woman?

WEEK 7

Name Change

SCRIPTURE READINGS:

Day One: Genesis 17:15-19 (God Changes Abram's Name)

Day Two: Psalm 126: 2 (Lots of Laughter)

Day Three: Job 8:21 (Laughter and Shouting)

Day Four: Genesis 21:16 (Sarah's Laughter)

Day Five: Proverbs 15:13 (Cheerful Spirit)

Day Six: Luke 6:21 (Weeping Turned to Laughter)

Day Seven: Psalm 32:11 (Be Glad in The Lord)

[15] "And God said unto Abraham, As for Sarai thy wife, thou shalt not call her name Sarai, but Sarah shall her name be.[16] And I will bless her, and give thee a son also of her: yea, I will bless her, and she shall be a mother of nations; kings of people shall be of her.[17] Then Abraham fell upon his face, and laughed, and said in his heart, Shall a child be born unto him that is an hundred years old? and shall Sarah, that is ninety years old, bear?[18] And Abraham said unto God, O that Ishmael might live before thee![19] And God said, Sarah thy wife shall bear thee a son indeed; and thou shalt call his name Isaac: and I will establish my covenant with him for an everlasting covenant, and with his seed after him." Genesis 17:15-19.

In the next chapter of Genesis, Genesis 17, God had a face-to-face, one-on-one meeting with Abram. By God's authority, Abram's name was changed to Abraham and his wife's name from Sarai to Sarah. God told Abraham that he would bless Sarah's barren womb and that she would have a child. God also told Abraham that many nations and kings would be brought forth from Sarah having a son, Isaac, in her old age.

Abraham actually laughed at God for saying that he would have a son at 100 years old and that Sarah would have a child when she was 90 years old. Luckily God didn't punish Abraham for laughing at His proclamation. Abraham wanted his other son Ishmael to be able to live under the Lord's blessing. The Lord acknowledged Abraham's laughter and then reassured him that he would have a son named Isaac in his old age.

The Lord also told Abraham that he would establish a covenant between Him and Isaac. Not just a covenant, but an *everlasting covenant* for Isaac and the many descendants that would come after him. The Lord then gave Abraham some more assurances and information about his soon-to-be-born son Isaac. Sarah would give birth to him at that same time in the next year. Then the Lord went up from Abraham and left him. It was exciting and awe-inspiring that God again came down from Heaven for a face-to-face conversation with Abraham.

He changed both his and his wife's name under His divine authority. This wasn't the only time that God had a face-to-face encounter with Abraham. There are many other instances of face-to-face encounters with God and Abraham in the Bible. Some are directly from God Himself, while others are from angels and messengers that God had sent to talk to Abraham and Sarah. God made His presence and authority clearly known to both Abraham and Sarah.

All women can learn a valuable and important lesson to trust God's authority over their lives. Remember, you don't have to go trudging through life on your own power. Instead, let God work in your life and see what can and will happen. If you let Him lead you while you follow His instructions, He will bless you in more ways than you can possibly fathom.

DISCUSSION QUESTIONS:

Have you ever wished for a face-to-face encounter with God?

____

____

____

____

____

Did you ever have a face-to-face or spiritual encounter with God?

____

____

____

____

____

Have you heard God speak to you? What did you say in response to Him?

____

____

____

____

____

JOURNAL QUESTIONS:

What would your reaction be if God had come to you for a face-to-face conversation about any children that you had or children that you longed for?

____

____

____

____

____

What would you say to Him? Would you be in shock, awe, and disbelief over the things He'd say?

____

____

____

____

____

Or would you take everything to heart and believe what God had just told you?

____

____

____

____

____

WEEK 8

Sarah Laughed

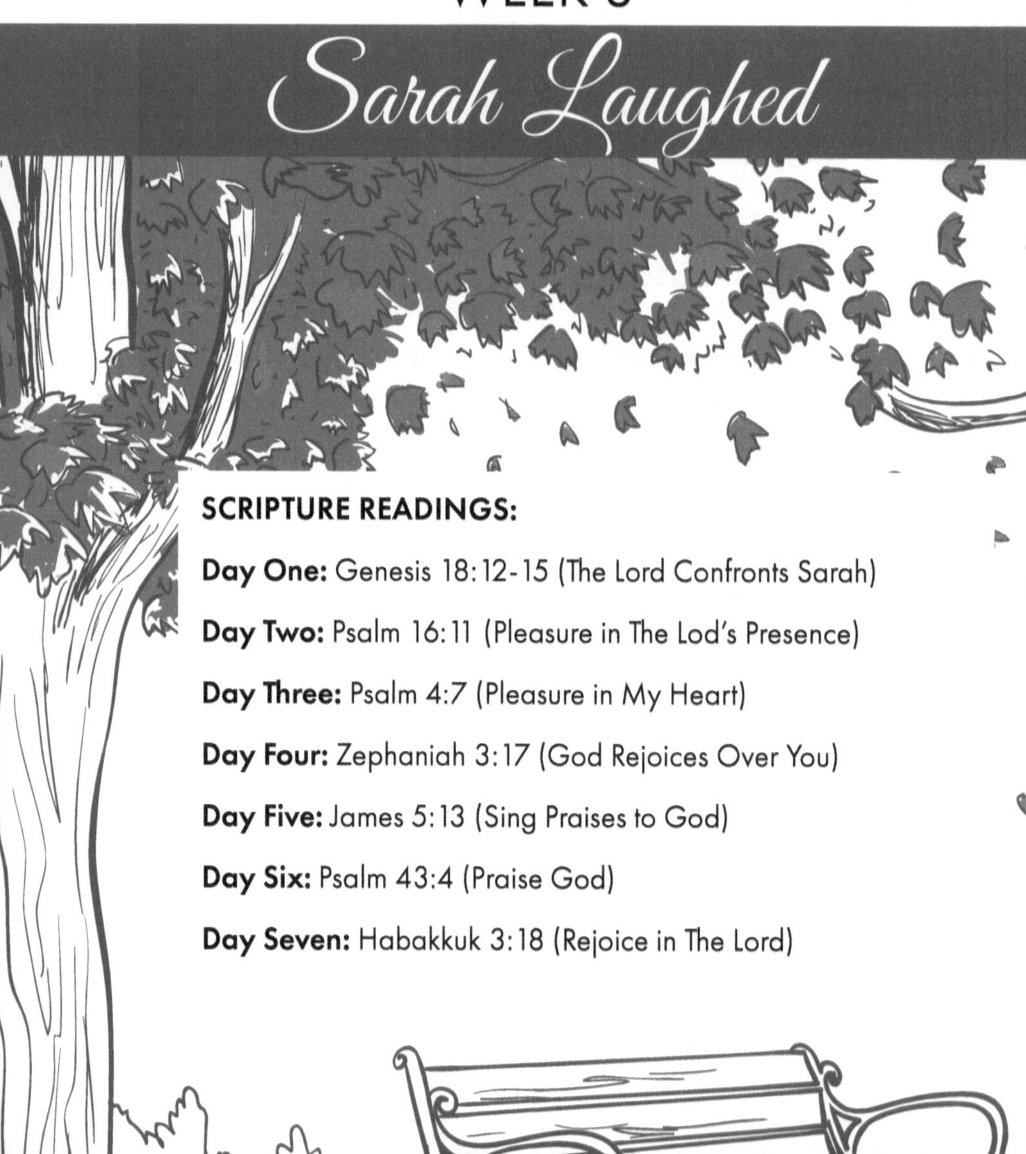

SCRIPTURE READINGS:

Day One: Genesis 18:12-15 (The Lord Confronts Sarah)

Day Two: Psalm 16:11 (Pleasure in The Lod's Presence)

Day Three: Psalm 4:7 (Pleasure in My Heart)

Day Four: Zephaniah 3:17 (God Rejoices Over You)

Day Five: James 5:13 (Sing Praises to God)

Day Six: Psalm 43:4 (Praise God)

Day Seven: Habakkuk 3:18 (Rejoice in The Lord)

¹² "Therefore Sarah laughed within herself, saying, After I am waxed old shall I have pleasure, my lord being old also?¹³ And the Lord said unto Abraham, Wherefore did Sarah laugh, saying, Shall I of a surety bear a child, which am old?¹⁴ Is anything too hard for the Lord? At the time appointed I will return unto thee, according to the time of life, and Sarah shall have a son.¹⁵ Then Sarah denied, saying, I laughed not; for she was afraid. And he said, Nay; but thou didst laugh."
Genesis 18: 12-15.

This chapter of Genesis is where things get even more interesting for Sarah and Abraham. Visitors came to Abraham and asked him where Sarah was. Abraham told the visitors that she was in the tent where they lived. One of the visitors told Abraham that he would return to Abraham for another visit by next year and that Sarah would have a son.

Sarah started listening to Abraham talking with the visitors. Both she and Abraham were very old, and Sarah was well past the age at which she could have any children. When she heard what they were saying to Abraham, she didn't believe it.

She actually laughed to herself at the thought of having a child in her old age. She thought to herself, "now that I'm old and so is my husband, now the Lord will grant me this gift?" Basically, it sounded as if she was saying, "oh, now the Lord cares about my prayer requests to have a child? Now that I'm old, I'll get to have a kid?" Any woman might be tempted to say that exact thing if she is over the age. She can get pregnant and then suddenly be told by a messenger of the Lord, or even a modern-day doctor, that she is, in fact, pregnant.

The Lord then came to Abraham and asked, "why did your wife Sarah laugh? Why did she laugh and say, "will I really have a child now that I'm old"? Is anything too hard for the Lord? I will return to you at this time next year. Sarah will have a son." Sarah was afraid because she had scoffed at the Lord's proclamation, so she flat out lied to God. She denied that she laughed about the Lord's proclamation.

Remember, God knows and sees all things, so He knew what Sarah's reaction would be before He even had the visitors come to tell Abraham the good news that he and Sarah would be parents after waiting for so long to have a child. He knew she'd laughed and confronted her about it. How terrifying it must have been for Sarah to be confronted by God Himself about laughing to herself about having a child. Any woman's reaction to that news might've been that of Sarah's. Women everywhere can learn to not take what the Lord tells them as a joke. Instead, they can rejoice with whatever the Lord tells them.

DISCUSSION QUESTIONS:

Have you ever heard your husband or boyfriend talking about your future together with God?

____

____

____

____

Have you ever laughed at the thought of having children? Have you prayed for the ability to have kids and have been discouraged when God didn't grant your request in the time you'd expected?

____

____

____

____

____

Did you ever react the same way Sarah did when you found out you were pregnant? Was your reaction shock and awe or denial?

____

____

____

____

____

Did you laugh, or were you praising and thanking Him for the blessing? Has God ever confronted you, asking why you didn't believe in His plan?

____

____

____

____

Is having a child at the forefront of your and your husband's mind?

____

____

____

____

____

What did you do when you found out you were going to have a child?

____

____

____

____

____

How old were you when you found out that you were pregnant?

____

____

____

____

____

WEEK 9

SCRIPTURE READINGS:

Day One: Colossians 3:6 (Sons of Disobedience)

Day Two: Ephesians 2:2 (Walking in Disobedience)

Day Three: 1 Samuel 15:23 (Rebellion and Insubordination)

Day Four: Titus 3:3 (We Were Once Foolish)

Day Five: Mathew 15:33 (Transgressors of God)

Day Six: Leviticus 26:18 (Warnings About Disobedience)

Day Seven: Romans 2:8 (Selfish Ambition)

"²⁴ Then the Lord rained upon Sodom and upon Gomorrah brimstone and fire from the Lord out of heaven;²⁵ And he overthrew those cities, and all the plain, and all the inhabitants of the cities, and that which grew upon the ground.²⁶ But his wife looked back from behind him, and she became a pillar of salt." Genesis 19:24-26.

Abraham's family had moved around in the Bible many times. When the Lord saw how wicked, immoral, and corrupt Sodom and Gomorrah had become, He intended to destroy those two cities. Abraham pleaded with God to spare his son Lot and his family because they lived in Sodom. The angels of the Lord came to Lot and warned him of the impending destruction of Sodom and Gomorrah. They also warned him to get anyone in his family out of that town before it was too late because God was merciful to Lot and his family. The angels told Lot to flee to the mountains, not stop anywhere on the plains, and not look back; otherwise, they would be swept away.

Lot was hesitant to do what the angels of the Lord were telling him and his family to do. Lot then pleaded with God and the angels asking if he could go to another small city nearby. He was afraid of going to the mountains because he was afraid he would die there. The Lord was again merciful and heard Lot's request and decided against destroying the town that Lot and his family were requesting to flee to. He then instructed them to go there quickly because He couldn't wipe out Sodom and Gomorrah until Lot and his family were safe in the town that was called Zoar.

God had told Lot and his family to go quickly and not look back as the cities were destroyed. The Lord rained down fire and brimstone out of heaven on Sodom and Gomorrah. However, Lot's wife disobeyed God. She looked back as the cities were being destroyed by God and His angels. Because she had disobeyed a direct order from God, she was then turned into a pillar of salt.

Women everywhere, listen up to what God says in this passage. He sent angels to Lot and his family, warning them to get out of Sodom because of how evil the people there had become. God warned Lot and his family to not stop anywhere along the journey to the new town they were going to. They even warned the entire family not to look back as the cities were being destroyed. However, it seems as though Satan had tempted Lot's wife to look back and made her want to see the destruction of God unfolding on the ungodly. When you get a direct order from God, obey it without question. Look at what happened to Lot's wife.

DISCUSSION QUESTIONS:

Have you ever received a direct order from God to go somewhere? What was your reaction to God telling you to move somewhere new?

Were you hesitant and trying to negotiate the way Lot did with the angels and God? Or did you listen to God without questions being asked?

What about God's direction made you think twice about following Him?

Have you ever been afraid of the things God had revealed to you in your life? How did you overcome your fears?

Where has God told you to go in your life? Did He tell you and your family to move to a new location for work purposes or to protect you and your family physically?

____

____

____

____

____

What lesson can you learn from this passage about following God's orders?

____

____

____

____

____

How can you do as God says without questioning Him or trying to negotiate with Him?

____

____

____

____

____

WEEK 10

Do Not Cross Dress

SCRIPTURE READINGS:

Day One: 1 Timothy 2:9-10 (Women Dress Wisely)

Day Two: Leviticus 20:13 (Sleeping with The Opposite Sex)

Day Three: Genesis 1:27 (God Created Man/Woman)

Day Four: 1 Corinthians 6:9 (Avoid Sexual Immorality)

Day Five: 1 Corinthians 6:19-20 (Your Body Is a Temple)

Day Six: Proverbs 31:30 (Charm Is Deceptive)

Day Seven: 1 Corinthians 10:31 (Do All Things for God)

"The woman shall not wear that which pertaineth unto a man, neither shall a man put on a woman's garment: for all that do so are abomination unto the Lord thy God." Deuteronomy 22:5

Have you ever been out on the town for the night with your family or friends and see a sight that you wish you could unsee- A woman dressing as a man or a man dressing as a woman? It says in the Bible that the Lord actually detests a person who dresses as the opposite sex or a person that is known as a crossdresser. It also says that dressing as the opposite sex is an abomination towards God. It warns you that as a woman, you should not dress as a man, and a man shouldn't dress as a woman.

Being told that it's an abomination to dress as someone of the opposite sex might seem harsh to you. It might seem as though it's a judgment upon people that happens all too often. But God gives you that stark warning to help you be aware of what's right and wrong in His sight. Dressing as the opposite sex is wrong in the Lord's sight. Therefore, you should refrain from doing it.

If you see someone you love dressing as a member of the opposite sex, you can calmly explain to them how God really feels about it. You can explain how God warns that it's wrong in His eyes. If they choose to listen to you and stop dressing as members of the opposite sex, they are trying not to sin.

However, if they choose not to listen to you and talk about how it's their own free will to dress the way they want to dress and that God shouldn't punish them for wearing what they want to wear, they are right thinking they have free will. God offers free will to everyone, but it's each individual's choice as to how they respond to having free will. They either obey God's commands, or they don't. It's entirely up to them.

You can pray they see the error of their ways and that God speaks to their heart about knowing the difference between right and wrong. If they see the error in their ways, they will stop doing wrong and ask for forgiveness from their sins. You can even pray for them and with them about repenting from their sins. You can be the one who guides them in the right direction to come before God and admit their sins and ask Him for forgiveness. Ask God to guide your words whenever you're around that person and pray for wisdom about how to approach them in the best way possible.

DISCUSSION QUESTIONS:

Have you ever seen a woman dressing as a man? Have you ever seen a man dressing as a woman? What was your reaction to seeing that?

____

____

____

____

Did this Bible passage open your eyes to the error of living life in that way? How did you approach someone who was okay with living in that type of lifestyle?

____

____

____

____

____

How did you show them the errors of their ways? How did you gently explain to them that their lifestyle choices aren't pleasing to God?

____

____

____

____

____

If you know someone who dresses as a man and is a woman, or if you know someone who is a woman that dresses as a man, how can you approach them with the kindness of God in your heart?

____

____

____

____

____

How can you kindly tell them about the sin that they are committing without seeming too judgmental?

____

____

____

____

____

How do you keep the friendship with that person if it's God's will that you should help them get out of their sinful life?

____

____

____

____

____

Rahab Hides the Spies

SCRIPTURE READINGS:

Day One: Luke 8:17 (Nothing Is Hidden)

Day Two: 2 Peter 3:9 (God Keeps His Promises)

Day Three: Isaiah 41:10 (God Is with You)

Day Four: Deuteronomy 28:1-2 (Obey God's Commands)

Day Five: Proverbs 18:10 (God's Strong Tower)

Day Six: Psalm 32:7 (Your Hiding Place)

Day Seven: Psalm 25:14 (Friendship of the Lord)

"⁴ And the woman took the two men, and hid them, and said thus, there came men unto me, but I wist not whence they were:⁵ And it came to pass about the time of shutting of the gate, when it was dark, that the men went out: whither the men went I wot not: pursue after them quickly; for ye shall overtake them.⁶ But she had brought them up to the roof of the house, and hid them with the stalks of flax, which she had laid in order upon the roof." Joshua 2:4-6

This Bible passage is the story of Rahab protecting and hiding the two Israelite spies from the men and the army of Jericho. Rahab willingly risked not only her own life but the lives of everyone in her family and the lives of the Israelite spies by offering them protection and putting them into hiding in the upper part of her roof when the soldiers of Jericho came looking for them.

She hid them and told the men of Jericho that the men had come to her, but she had no idea as to where they might be hiding. She also told the men in Jericho's army that the spies from Israel left when it was dark. She told the men in Jericho's army to go after them quickly so that the Israelite spies could be captured and brought to justice. However, she had told them to pursue the Israelite spies to get them away from her house and keep the men in Jericho's army from searching her home.

No doubt she was afraid for her and her family's life. She was also scared for the Israelites' lives. She didn't want them to be found and executed because she was a righteous woman who believed in the promises of God. She knew if the spies were found, they would be executed, and if they found out, she was not only lying to the men in Jericho's army about not knowing where the spies had gone but the fact that she was also hiding them in the roof of her house, she and her entire family would be killed as well. She knew the risks that she was taking were enormous.

But she also knew the rewards of obeying what God had instructed her to do. She wanted to do the right thing, even if it meant risking her life and even the Israelites life. She knew the Israelites were going to overthrow Jericho and knock down its walls by the power of God. For Rahab, the rewards outweighed the risks, no matter if she and her family's lives were all at stake or not.

Even if it meant that she and her family would get killed, she knew she had to hide the spies. She hid them in the upper part of her roof, where most people wouldn't think to look. God had made her a sagacious person to know how to make the spies hiding place look like a natural part of the roof.

Have you ever risked your life to do what God had commanded you? Have you ever risked your and your family's life to keep someone safe?

How did God tell you to act on His plan? What was the result of you obeying God?

Did you ever think about turning back to save your own life, or did you press on with courage like Rahab did?

JOURNAL QUESTIONS:

Have you ever risked your life and hid someone to help someone get God's message across?

____

____

____

____

____

Have you ever put your life or your family's life in danger to protect some-one trying to carry out a plan from God?

____

____

____

____

____

Did anyone found out about you protecting someone else? Were you afraid but determined to do the right thing like Rahab?

____

____

____

____

____

Rahab Pleads with The Two Spies

SCRIPTURE READINGS:

Day One: Mathew 5:33-37 (Don't Swear Falsely)

Day Two: Numbers 23:19 (God Is God)

Day Three: Ecclesiastes 5:1-2 (Speak Less)

Day Four: Psalm 15:2-5 (Fear the Lord)

Day Five: Leviticus 5:4 (Do Not Say Rash Promises)

Day Six: James 5:12 (Let Your Yes Be Yes)

Day Seven: Ecclesiastes 5:5 (Do Not Vow Before God)

"⁹ And she said unto the men, I know that the Lord hath given you the land, and that your terror is fallen upon us, and that all the inhabitants of the land faint because of you... ¹² Now therefore, I pray you, swear unto me by the Lord, since I have shewed you kindness, that ye will also shew kindness unto my father's house, and give me a true token: And that ye will save alive my father, and my mother, and my brethren, and my sisters, and all that they have, and deliver our lives from death. Joshua 2: 9-10, 12

The story of Rahab helping the spies continues with Rahab actually going to talk to the men and help them escape with their lives. She tells the men that she knows it is in God's plan to get the land of Jericho. She also explains that much fear has overtaken the people in Jericho because they had all heard how the Israelites were led by God through the Red Sea and how God parted the Red Sea so the Israelites could escape from Pharaoh and his soldiers after being freed from slavery in Egypt.

She also told them that everyone in Jericho knew what the Israelites had done to the two Amorite kings, Shihon and Og. She knew that they had utterly destroyed the two kings. The news that the Israelites had killed the two Amorite kings had traveled quickly throughout the land of Jericho. She also proclaimed that God was the ruler of all on Earth and in Heaven. She then made the two spies from Israel swear to her under God and by His power alone that the two Israelite spies that she kept safe would look upon her and her family with favor because she and her family had risked their lives to hide and protect them. She wanted a sure sign that the Israelite men would be kind to her and look upon her and her family with favor from God because she had shown them love and kindness.

After what Rahab had done for the men, no one could blame her for asking for the Israelite spies to return her favor of kindness. No one could blame her for asking for the men to look upon her and her family with favor. No one could blame her for wanting her favor to be returned. She was allowed to ask for the favor to be returned by the Israelites. She knew a lot about them, so she figured that she may as well tell them how fast word about the Israelites deliverance from Egypt and how powerful God was, had gotten around.

She was a woman who was determined to do God's good work no matter the risk, and then she professed her acknowledgment of who God was and is to the Israelite spies. Her faith remained unshakable even in her most dangerous and desperate moments of protecting the spies. She wasn't afraid to profess her knowledge of God to the Israelite spies. She wasn't scared to do the right thing or afraid to be brave enough to ask for her favor to be returned.

Were you ever put in a position where you had to risk your life and your safety to help someone else?

____

____

____

____

____

What did you do in that situation? Did you take the direction from God and act right away, or did you hesitate to act?

____

____

____

____

____

Did you ask for the favor to be returned while proclaiming how good God is?

____

____

____

____

____

Have you ever risked your life to help someone in need? What did God tell you to do in that situation?

____

____

____

____

____

____

Did you act immediately or freeze up in fear? Were you bold enough to ask the person you helped to return the favor?

____

____

____

____

____

____

WEEK 13

SCRIPTURE READINGS:

Day One: James 1:2-5 (Faith Produces Character)

Day Two: Romans 8:28 (God Works All Things for Good)

Day Three: Mathew 5:34-37 (Do Not Take an Oath)

Day Four: Mathew 5:33: (Do What You Said You Would Do)

Day Five: Psalm 89:34 (Don't Altar Your Covenant)

Day Six: James 1:12 (Remain Steadfast During Trials)

Day Seven: Ecclesiastes 5:4 (Honor your Vow Before God)

"And the men answered her, Our life for yours, if ye utter not this our business. And it shall be, when the Lord hath given us the land, that we will deal kindly and truly with thee.[15] Then she let them down by a cord through the window: for her house was upon the town wall, and she dwelt upon the wall.[16] And she said unto them, Get you to the mountain, lest the pursuers meet you; and hide yourselves there three days, until the pursuers be returned: and afterward may ye go your way.[17] And the men said unto her, We will be blameless of this thine oath which thou hast made us swear." Joshua 2: 14-17

The two spies and Rahab continued to talk. They finally spoke up and assured her that she and her family would be kept safe. They even said, "our life for yours." They said if Rahab agreed to keep what they were doing a secret and if she didn't tell anyone what they were doing, they promised that they would treat Rahab and her entire family with the same kindness she had bestowed upon them.

Then she let them down by a rope in her window. The cool fact about Rahab's house was that it was actually part of the city of Jericho's wall. She then told the spies to run to the hills so none of the men of Jericho would find them. She told them to stay there and stay hidden there for at least three days until the men of the army of Jericho had returned. When three days passed, then it would be safe for them to go on their way again.

As they were leaving, the two spies warned her that if she talked about hiding them, they would deny being in her house if they were captured. They said that the oath and promise she had made them promise for her and her entire family's safety would be a lost cause if she ratted them out and told the men in Jericho's army where they went, were going, and where they were hiding.

The spies weren't afraid to tell her what would happen to her if she ever ratted them out or told anyone in Jericho what they were doing. They were going to overthrow the city of Jericho. Whether she liked it or not, Rahab had volunteered herself into that plan that God had developed for the Israelites. Rahab knew she couldn't ever tell anyone what she knew or ever tell anyone that she had helped the two spies.

God protected her and her family because she did the right thing. You, too, can do the right thing and keep something that is said in confidence a secret between you, God, and the other person. There's no shame in not repeating what someone told you in confidence. It actually helps you establish a better, more trustworthy relationship with that person. Rahab was honorable when she didn't repeat the plans of the Israelites to anyone in Jericho. The two spies were also honorable in saying that as long as Rahab kept her word, they would have no problem keeping their word.

DISCUSSION QUESTIONS:

Were you ever told something by a friend in confidence? What was your reaction to your friend's confession?

____

____

____

____

____

Did you keep their secrets confidential between the two of you like Rahab did of the spies' whereabouts and their plans, or did you talk about them with other people?

____

____

____

____

____

God wants you to honor your friend and keep whatever they said to you private, just between you, God, and the other person.

____

____

____

____

____

Did you keep the things a friend said to you confidential, like Rahab?

____

____

____

____

____

____

What can you learn from her conversation with the spies?

____

____

____

____

____

____

____

WEEK 14

SCRIPTURE READINGS:

Day One: Proverbs 11:3 (Crookedness of The Treacherous)

Day Two: Ephesians 4:31-32 (Be Kind to Everyone)

Day Three: Colossians 3:9 (Do Not Lie To One Another)

Day Four: 1 John 4:1 (Test Each Spirit)

Day Five: James 4:1 (Our Passions Are at War)

Day Six: Judges 16:4-6 (Delilah Tries to Find Samson's Secrets)

Day Seven: Proverbs 24:28 (Testifying Against Your Neighbor)

"That he told her all his heart, and said unto her, There hath not come a razor upon mine head; for I have been a Nazarite unto God from my mother's womb: if I be shaven, then my strength will go from me, and I shall become weak, and be like any other man.[18] And when Delilah saw that he had told her all his heart, she sent and called for the lords of the Philistines, saying, Come up this once, for he hath shewed me all his heart. Then the lords of the Philistines came up unto her, and brought money in their hand.[19] And she made him sleep upon her knees; and she called for a man, and she caused him to shave off the seven locks of his head; and she began to afflict him, and his strength went from him." Judges 16: 17-19

Samson was a warrior of God. He was the strongest man in the Bible and could tear off a donkey's jaw bone and then beat a man to death with the donkey's jawbone. He started dating a woman named Delilah. She was told by the Philistine army to lure Samson into sharing his secret for his superhuman strength with her. They wanted to know the secret to his Godly and superhuman strength so they could take it all from him and kill him. She agreed and plotted with them against Samson.

Three times he gave her false information about the source of his strength. Three times she tried to take his superhuman strength away from him. You would have thought that he would have figured out that she was devising a plan and scheming with her people against him after the first or second time. Apparently, Samson loved Delilah so much that he was blinded by his love for her. He was so blinded by his love for her that he thought she actually loved him back when in reality, she was only sleeping with him to take away his strength. She was merely using him for her own selfish desires.

She didn't think Samson actually loved her because he had not been giving her a straight answer about where his strength had actually come from. Three times she tried to get him to open up to her and to trust her, and to tell her where his strength had come from. Samson may have known she was deceptive in her motives and that she was plotting against him. If God had warned him of Delilah's deception, he really should have listened to God instead of being head over heels with someone who clearly didn't love him.

Finally, he ended up spilling the beans and telling her about his strength. He told her that he had never used a razor to cut his head before, that he was born a Nazarite who was dedicated to God his entire life. He also told her that if anyone shaved his head, he would lose his strength. She went behind his back once again and told the philistines she had discovered Samson's secret. She was paid 20 pieces of silver and had another man cut off Samson's hair while he was asleep on her lap! Talk about deception. Don't do what Delilah did to Samson. Honor your boyfriend or husband.

Have you ever plotted against your boyfriend or husband?

____

____

____

____

____

____

Did he find out about your plot? What was his reaction when he found out about your deception?

____

____

____

____

____

____

____

Have you ever thought your husband was keeping secrets from you? Have you ever wanted to find out about one of your husband's secrets?

____

____

____

____

____

____

Did you plot against him? Did you plot against him alone or with help from other people? What was your reaction to finding out the secrets?

____

____

____

____

____

____

Ruth Stays with Naomi

SCRIPTURE READINGS:

Day One: Psalm 34:18 (Close to The Broken Hearted)

Day Two: 2 Corinthians 5:8 (Be of Good Courage)

Day Three: John 14:27 (Peace of God)

Day Four: Isaiah 54:10 (God's Steadfast Love)

Day Five: Proverbs 17:17 (Friends Forever)

Day Six: Hebrews 12:1 (Cloud of Witnesses)

Day Seven: 2 Corinthians 5:6 (Walk by Faith)

[14] And they lifted up their voice, and wept again: and Orpah kissed her mother-
in-law; but Ruth clave unto her... And Ruth said, Intreat me not to leave thee, or
to return from following after thee: for whither thou goest, I will go; and where
thou lodgest, I will lodge: thy people shall be my people, and thy God my God:
[17] Where thou diest, will I die, and there will I be buried: The Lord do so to me, and
more also, if ought but death part thee and me." Ruth 1:14-17

You have probably all heard the story of Ruth and her mother-in-law Naomi. Naomi had two sons, and they were married to Orpah and Ruth. Sometime later, both of their husbands died, as did Naomi's husband. Naomi had advised her two daughters-in-law to go back to their home countries because they had no reason to stay with her anymore now that both of her sons were dead. At first, they refused to leave Naomi's side. But after much convincing, Orpah decided that she would return to her homeland and be among her people again. This is where the passage that we are discussing begins.

They lifted up their voices to God and wept with each other once again. Orpah kissed Naomi and left to return to her homeland and be among her people after many years of being away from them. But not Ruth. Rather than leave Naomi to fend for herself, she stayed by Naomi's side and clung to her. She then professed her love for Naomi and her trust in God. She said to Naomi, "please don't leave me or tell me to abandon you. Wherever you go, I will too, go with you. Where you go, I will follow you. Where you stay, I will stay. Your people will be my people, and your God will be and is my God. Where you die, I will die, and where you are buried, I too will be buried beside you. The Lord can do what He wants with me. Only death shall part you and me, Naomi!"

Talk about being dedicated to someone and loyal to someone that she loved dearly. Ruth didn't want to leave Naomi or abandon her. Instead, Ruth wanted to stay with her, protect her, and love her throughout her journey to a new land. Ladies everywhere can take this cue from Ruth- if you love someone, tell them. If God is telling you not to leave them hanging, then listen to God's instructions and don't ever leave them hanging high and dry in any circumstance.

Rather than walk away from someone you love, ask God to show you how to behave like Ruth did to Naomi and have unwavering loyalty and love towards the person. Ruth was willing to do anything and everything to stick with Naomi. She was ready to die and be buried next to Naomi, too, and said death would be the only thing that separated them.

DISCUSSION QUESTIONS:

Have you ever been told by a relative or a friend to leave them and return to your old way of life?

____

____

____

____

Have you ever been as loyal to a friend or family member as Ruth was to her mother-in-law Naomi? Did you ever say that death would be the only thing that would separate you from a friend or family member?

____

____

____

____

How can you show your friend or family member that you're with them for the long haul, through good and evil, no matter what may come?

____

____

____

____

How can you show your family member or friend true loyalty just like Ruth did for Naomi?

____

____

____

____

____

What things can you say to them to let them know that you're not ever going to leave their side no matter what may happen?

____

____

____

____

____

WEEK 16

SCRIPTURE READINGS:

Day One: Ruth 2:2-3 (Ruth's Plan)

Day Two: Ruth 2:5-6 (Take Advice from Family)

Day Three: Philippians 1:3 (Thank God in Remembrance)

Day Four: 1 Corinthians 15:58 (Your Labor is Not in Vain)

Day Five: 1 Corinthians 6:14 (God will Raise You in Power)

Day Six: Romans 12:8 (Work Generously)

Day Seven: Psalm 90:17 (God Establishes the Work of Your Hands)

"And Ruth the Moabitess said unto Naomi, Let me now go to the field, and glean ears of corn after him in whose sight I shall find grace. And she said unto her, Go, my daughter.[3] And she went, and came, and gleaned in the field after the reapers: and her hap was to light on a part of the field belonging unto Boaz, who was of the kindred of Elimelech. Then said Boaz unto his servant that was set over the reapers, Whose damsel is this? [6] And the servant that was set over the reapers answered and said, It is the Moabitish damsel that came back with Naomi out of the country of Moab." Ruth 2:2-3, 5-6.

In the next chapter of Ruth, Ruth and Naomi have journeyed back to Naomi's home country. Ruth was a Moabite. She came to Naomi and told her that she would go into the field and pick up the ears of corn from whoever showed respect and grace to her. Naomi agreed with Ruth and told her to go. Ruth then went and gleaned in the field after the reapers and workers. To glean mean to collect gradually, bit by bit. As it turned out, Ruth was working in a field that belonged to Boaz.

When Boaz arrived, he greeted the harvesters saying, "peace be with you!" The workers then answered him, saying, "The Lord bless you!" When he noticed Ruth, he asked one of his head workers who she was. He also asked his head overseer who Ruth belonged to. The person told him that Ruth was the Moabite who came from Moab with Naomi.

Ruth was already brave enough to leave her home country for a long time when she married Naomi's son. Then she was braver still when she expressed her love, loyalty, and devotion to Naomi and said that she would never leave Naomi's side. To journey with Naomi to a new land with no income source and be brave enough to go out among other workers in a field to pick up what the workers in the field had left behind took a lot of courage. Ruth was a fearless and courageous woman. To go into a field of workers where she wasn't known, to see if she could find favor with the person who owned the field, was a significant risk to take.

She could have ended up in a field where the workers and the overseer told her to leave. She could have been hurt by the other workers when they found out she was a Moabite. She could have been mistreated by the owner of the field when he found out who she was. Instead of all of those scenarios happening, Boaz asked his workers who she was. He was curious about her and wanted to learn more about her.

God must have been telling Ruth and leading her to work in Boaz's field because He knew she would find favor in his eyes. You, too, can be like Ruth and go out in faith to do the work that God is calling you to do. Trust in His timing and His plan for your life.

Have you ever wanted to go where God was calling you, even though you weren't sure where He was leading you?

____

____

____

____

____

Have you ever told a family member about your plan to work in a new environment? What was their reaction to your plan?

____

____

____

____

____

____

Have you ever worked in a new place? Did you feel God leading you to work there?

____

____

____

____

____

Did your family agree with you and tell you to do what your heart was telling you to do?

____

____

____

____

____

Did you trust God like Ruth when she stepped out in faith and had courage when she went to work in Boaz's field?

____

____

____

____

____

SCRIPTURE READINGS:

Day One: Romans 12:11 (Be Faithful in Zeal)

Day Two: Proverbs 16:13 (Commit Your Plans to God)

Day Three: 1 Timothy 5:8 (Provide for Your Relatives)

Day Four: 2 Timothy 2:6 (First Share of Crops)

Day Five: 2 Thessalonians 3:10-12 (Be Willing to Work)

Day Six: Proverbs 12:24 (Be Diligent)

Day Seven: 1 Thessalonians 4:11-12 (Live Quietly)

⁸"Then said Boaz unto Ruth, Hearest thou not, my daughter? Go not to glean in another field, neither go from hence, but abide here fast by my maidens: ⁹ Let thine eyes be on the field that they do reap, and go thou after them: have I not charged the young men that they shall not touch thee? and when thou art athirst, go unto the vessels, and drink of that which the young men have drawn. Then she fell on her face, and bowed herself to the ground, and said unto him, Why have I found grace in thine eyes, that thou shouldest take knowledge of me, seeing I am a stranger?"

Ruth 2: 8-10

Then the overseer told Moab that Ruth had requested that they let her glean in Boaz's field. He told him that she had been working from early morning until the afternoon and hadn't stopped gathering corn the entire day except for a short rest in the shelter. Boaz then approached Ruth and told her that she was allowed to work any time in his field. He even advised her not to go into another person's field because he would be fair to her and give her more than enough food to eat. He also advised her to follow along after the other women who worked in his field and gather up as much food as she wanted. He then told her that the men in the field wouldn't lay a hand on her because he told them not to harm her. He even invited her to go get a drink of water any time she was thirsty, no matter the time of day.

Ruth was amazed at Boaz and his words, not to mention his kindness, and she fell at his feet, bowing before him, telling him thank you. She then asked him why he was so kind to her because he didn't even know her, and she was a stranger to him. She asked him why he had shown her such grace, compassion, and kindness.

God must have known that Boaz would treat Ruth with compassion, humility, and kindness. He didn't have to let her glean in the fields, but he did. Boaz didn't have to be friendly and tell her that she could get a drink whenever she was thirsty. He also didn't have to protect her from the men who worked in his field, but he did. It's no wonder Ruth bowed before him, thanking him for his kindness and compassion. Whenever someone shows you compassion and empathy, you can show them respect back. You can also tell them thank you, just as Ruth told Boaz, "thank you."

You can then return the favor of their kindness whenever the time presents itself to you. Pray and ask God to show you ways that you can return the kindness that person showed you. Remember, God led Ruth to Boaz's field for His reason and His reason alone. God was taking care of her before she even set foot in Boaz's field. Ruth trusted God that she would be safe among the workers, and she was blessed immensely by God with being able to work in Boaz's field.

DISCUSSION QUESTIONS:

Have you ever found favor in someone's eyes, whether it was a neighbor, an extended family member, an old friend, or a new supervisor at your job?

____

____

____

____

____

How did that person treat you with kindness? What was your reaction to being showed such kindness?

____

____

____

____

____

Were you amazed and thankful like Ruth was, or did you take the person's kindness for granted?

____

____

____

____

____

How did you repay that person's kindness? How did the person's kindness affect your life, your work situation?

____

____

____

____

____

Did the person's compassion even affect your family life or your faith?

____

____

____

____

____

How did God show you His hand was and is upon everything you do in life?

____

____

____

____

____

WEEK 18

Boaz Talks with Ruth

SCRIPTURE READINGS:

Day One: Proverbs 31:26 (Be Kind to Everyone)

Day Two: Proverbs 11:17 (Kindness is Blessed)

Day Three: Colossians 3:12 (Have A Compassionate Heart)

Day Four: Proverbs 19:17 (Give to The Poor)

Day Five: Romans 11:22 (Kindness and Severity of God)

Day Six: Acts 20:35 (Better to Give Than to Receive)

Day Seven: Micah 6:8 (Walk Humbly with God)

[11] "And Boaz answered and said unto her, It hath fully been shewed me, all that thou hast done unto thy mother-in-law since the death of thine husband: and how thou hast left thy father and thy mother, and the land of thy nativity, and art come unto a people which thou knewest not heretofore. [12] The Lord recompense thy work, and a full reward be given thee of the Lord God of Israel, under whose wings thou art come to trust." Ruth 2:11-12

Boaz then explained to Ruth that he had heard all about the wonderful thing she had done for her mother-in-law Naomi. He knew all about Ruth giving up going back to her home land and deciding to go wherever Naomi went. He knew that Naomi had two sons and that they both died. He knew that Ruth had journeyed to a land where no one knew her. He also said that he hoped the Lord would bless her richly for the kindness she had shown her mother-in-law and that he hoped the Lord would repay her for the blessing she was to Naomi.

He knew that Ruth was a believer in God and knew that she trusted Him with all her heart. He even called Him the God of Israel, so Ruth knew that he was the real deal among many people in the land. She knew she had come to the right field to work. God led her to go to Boaz's field so she would be safe from harm, have more food and clean water than she ever imagined or hoped for. God also led her to work in Boaz's field because He knew that he would show great kindness and compassion to her.

God knew that Boaz knew all about Ruth and how she stayed with Naomi even though she didn't have to. How do you think Boaz knew all of that information about Ruth and her life? It wasn't just because she had been talked about all over town. It was because God had also told Boaz about her in ways that only He could have told him.

Ruth was blessed exponentially by Boaz's words and by his kindness. She probably wasn't expecting him to know so much about her, her past life, her husband, and how she left her mother and father to be with her husband, Naomi's son. She probably didn't know that the people in the town and even Boaz's overseers knew as much about her as they did. She also probably wasn't expecting Boaz to be as kind as he was to her by allowing her to gather as much food as she wanted. Even though she might have been shocked that Boaz knew so much about her life, maybe in her heart, she was glad that he knew a lot about her.

A word of advice to all women- the word about your life travels fast, so always make sure you're showing kindness to everyone you encounter, just as Ruth did to Boaz and his workers.

DISCUSSION QUESTIONS:

Were you ever blessed by your boss or supervisor at your job? In what ways did he or she bless you?

____

____

____

____

____

Had your boss ever told you that he or she knew about the nice things you'd done on the job or for your former coworkers at your last job?

____

____

____

____

____

What was your reaction to hearing that your boss knew of some of the nice things you'd done for other people?

____

____

____

____

____

How were you blessed by a boss or even a colleague at your job? In what areas of work were you blessed by this person?

____

____

____

____

____

____

Have you ever had a boss tell you that he or she knew of kind things you'd done in the past?

____

____

____

____

____

____

SCRIPTURE READINGS:

Day One: Mathew 25:34-36 (Inherit God's Kingdom)

Day Two: 2 Peter 1:7 (Approach Everyone with Brotherly Love)

Day Three: Romans 15:2 (Build Your Neighbor Up)

Day Four: Proverbs 21:21 (Pursue Righteousness)

Day Five: Acts 28:2 (Unusual Acts of Kindness)

Day Six: 2 Thessalonians 3:13 (Don't Grow Tired of Doing Good)

Day Seven: 1 Peter 3:8-9 (Be A Blessing)

[14]"And Boaz said unto her, At mealtime come thou hither, and eat of the bread, and dip thy morsel in the vinegar. And she sat beside the reapers: and he reached her parched corn, and she did eat, and was sufficed, and left. [15] And when she was risen up to glean, Boaz commanded his young men, saying, Let her glean even among the sheaves, and reproach her not: [16] And let fall also some of the handfuls of purpose for her, and leave them, that she may glean them, and rebuke her not. [17] So she gleaned in the field until even, and beat out that she had gleaned: and it was about an ephah of barley. [18] And she took it up, and went into the city: and her mother in law saw what she had gleaned: and she brought forth, and gave to her that she had reserved after she was sufficed." Ruth 2:14-18

Ruth again expressed her gratitude to Boaz for his kindness as the chapter goes on. She told Boaz that he had put her mind at ease by being kind to her even though she wasn't one of the people who worked in his field as one of his servants. Boaz then showed even more kindness to Ruth by telling her to join him at mealtime and inviting her to try the bread with wine vinegar. She sat next to the harvesters, and Boaz offered her roasted grain. When she had enough to eat, she even had food leftover. She got up to go back to work in the field. Boaz then commanded his young men to let Ruth eat and glean among the sheaves. He told them to not reprimand her. He wanted them to leave some stalks out from the actual wheat bundles to take those for food for her and Naomi.

Not very many people would be so generous to a woman that they had just met. But Boaz was very different and unique. He had seen that Ruth was not like other women. He knew she was special in God's eyes and favored in His eyes, so he knew he had to treat her fairly.

Ruth worked in the fields until evening had come. Then she counted the barley she had gathered, and it was around eight bushels. As she carried it all back to town, her mother-in-law had seen how much she had gathered only in one day, and she was astonished. Ruth had also brought her what she had eaten and had leftovers from her dinner with Boaz. They both had more than enough food at that time, and they were both blessed and knew they wouldn't go hungry as long as Ruth continued to work in Boaz's field.

Ruth knew how fortunate she was to be working in Boaz's field. In that day and age, for any woman to be treated with compassion, humility, honor, and respect was a true gift from God. Ruth didn't take working in the field for granted, even though she worked in Boaz's field, where she was treated differently. She knew she had to work in the field to get enough food to eat. Ruth was just doing what the Lord had told her to do, so God was blessing her in more ways than one.

Were you ever invited to a fancy dinner with your boss or a fancy company outing where you were invited to sit at your boss's table?

____

____

____

____

____

____

Did they offer you amazing food and drinks? Did you have more food and drinks than you ever expected to?

____

____

____

____

____

____

What was that experience like for you?

____

____

____

____

____

____

What was your reaction when your boss invited you to eat with them? Did you take the invite as an honor?

____

____

____

____

____

____

Did your boss's treatment change the way you worked?

____

____

____

____

____

____

WEEK 20

SCRIPTURE READINGS:

Day One: Genesis 1:27-28 (First Marriage of The Bible)

Day Two: Malachi 2:14-15 (Be Faithful in Marriage)

Day Three: Colossians 3:14 (Put on Love)

Day Four: Ecclesiastes 4:9 (Two Are Better Than One)

Day Five: Ephesians 5:25 (Husbands Love Your Wives)

Day Six: Genesis 2:24 (Leave Your Mother and Father)

Day Seven: Mark 10:9 (What God Has Joined Together)

⁹"And Boaz said unto the elders, and unto all the people, Ye are witnesses this day, that I have bought all that was Elimelech's, and all that was Chilion's and Mahlon's, of the hand of Naomi.¹⁰ Moreover Ruth the Moabitess, the wife of Mahlon, have I purchased to be my wife, to raise up the name of the dead upon his inheritance, that the name of the dead be not cut off from among his brethren, and from the gate of his place: ye are witnesses this day.¹¹ And all the people that were in the gate, and the elders, said, We are witnesses. The Lord make the woman that is come into thine house like Rachel and like Leah, which two did build the house of Israel: and do thou worthily in Ephratah, and be famous in Bethlehem. And let thy house be like the house of Pharez, whom Tamar bare unto Judah, of the seed which the Lord shall give thee of this young woman." Ruth 4:9-12

In the last chapter of Ruth, Boaz made an announcement to the people. He told them that he had purchased the property of Elimelek, Kilion, and Mahlon from Ruth's mother-in-law Naomi. He also told the crowd that he had acquired her daughter-in-law Ruth and that he would marry her. He wanted to keep Ruth and her husband's name, Mahlon's name, within the dead men's property. He also didn't want their name to go away from them among his family or his hometown.

The many witnesses blessed their marriage. They even said, "may Ruth be like Rachel and Leah who together have built up the family of Israel." They hoped and prayed for Boaz and Ruth to be famous in Bethlehem and in all of Ephrathah. The crowd gave their blessing on any children Boaz and Ruth would have. They said they hoped that Boaz and Ruth's family would be like Perez, the son Tamar had with Judah. Ruth and Boaz must have been happy that the crowd had given them their warm wishes and prayed for blessings to come upon them in their new marriage. Ruth also must have been thrilled that everyone prayed for her to be like Rachel and Leah.

Rachel and Leah were the wives of Jacob. Ruth must have been delighted that she was marrying Boaz and that everyone in the town accepted her as his new wife. To have the townspeople readily accept her and pray for blessing to be bestowed upon her was a big deal. What was even a bigger deal was that they hoped she would have many children and that they would bless both her and Boaz's life. She also must have been thrilled that her family name would not be forgotten, thanks to Boaz. For a man, she had met in the fields to marry her and publicly announce it was a big deal in those days.

When your marriage is ordained by God, you will feel peace in your soul, body, and in your mind. You will feel the peace that surpasses all human understanding. You will feel genuine Godly, true love for your spouse, and your connection will be with each other and with God Himself. Ask God to bless your marriage the way God blessed and ordained Boaz's and Ruth's.

Do you think your marriage is ordained by God? How can you tell if it's ordained by Him?

____

____

____

____

____

____

Do you feel His peace in your marriage? Have you prayed for your husband to know God on a personal level?

____

____

____

____

____

____

Have you ever prayed for your future spouse to be led to you by God? Are you still waiting for "the one" in your life?

____

____

____

____

____

____

Are you discouraged when you aren't making progress towards dating or marriage?

____

____

____

____

____

____

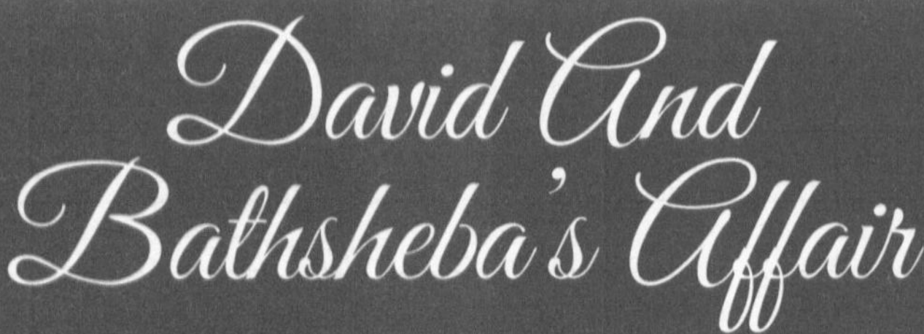

David And Bathsheba's Affair

SCRIPTURE READINGS:

Day One: Hebrews 13:4 (God is Judge)

Day Two: Proverbs 6:32 (Don't Commit Adultery)

Day Three: Mathew 5:27-28 (Lust Is Adultery)

Day Four: Leviticus 20:10 (Warnings About Adultery)

Day Five: Mathew 5:32 (Don't Divorce Your Wife)

Day Six: 1 Corinthians 10:13 (Resist Temptations)

Day Seven: James 4:17 (Know and Do What Is Right)

"And it came to pass in an evening tide, that David arose from off his bed, and walked upon the roof of the king's house: and from the roof he saw a woman washing herself; and the woman was very beautiful to look upon.[3] And David sent and enquired after the woman. And one said, Is not this Bathsheba, the daughter of Eliam, the wife of Uriah the Hittite?[4] And David sent messengers, and took her; and she came in unto him, and he lay with her; for she was purified from her uncleanness: and she returned unto her house.[5] And the woman conceived, and sent and told David, and said, I am with child." 2 Samuel 11: 2-5

David was one of the wisest kings in all of the Bible. But he also made many mistakes in his life. Just like everyone on Earth, David sinned. In this particular instance, he committed adultery by lusting after and sleeping with a married woman named Bathsheba. David saw her bathing on the rooftop of her home in the moonlight one evening when he got up from his bed and walked onto his roof. He was automatically smitten by her and her beauty, so he sent some messengers to find out about Bathsheba.

Through his messengers, he found out that she was married to Uriah, the Hittite serving in David's army. David sent messengers to take Bathsheba and bring her to him. Here is where the adultery happened- David then slept with Bathsheba. She was being purified from her monthly period, and then she went back home. Later on, she came back and told David the shocking news that she was pregnant.

David not only had lustful feelings for Bathsheba when she was legally married to Uriah. He also wanted to sleep with her and have her for his own because she was so beautiful in his eyes. Not only did David break one of the commandments, but so did Bathsheba. She knew in her heart that she was married to Uriah and that she shouldn't sleep with David. One, because it was wrong, and two, because he was the king and she was a peasant woman. Instead of sending David's messengers away from her and telling them to leave her alone, she agreed to come to him.

She also let herself go when she agreed to sleep with him. She let the thought of her marriage to Uriah pretty much be thrown out the window when she agreed to sleep with David. So, you can imagine her shock when she found out she was pregnant with David's child.

What would David do? Would he destroy her or tell her to abort the child? After all, he was the king at that time. Even worse, what would her husband Uriah do when he found out that she was pregnant and the baby wasn't his? God commanded people to not commit adultery (see Exodus 20). Let this be a lesson for all women: do not cheat on your husbands, no matter how nice the other man is. You're supposed to be loyal to your husband and the vows you made to him and God in marriage.

Have you ever been tempted to be with someone who isn't your husband?

____

____

____

____

Have you ever had sex with someone other than your husband? What did you learn from that experience?

____

____

____

____

____

Did your husband find out about your infidelity? What was his reaction when you told him the truth?

____

____

____

____

____

Did he forgive you, or did he automatically call a divorce lawyer?

____

____

____

____

____

JOURNAL QUESTIONS:

Have you ever cheated on your husband? What were the consequences of your choice?

____

____

____

____

Did you get pregnant with the person who wasn't your husband?

____

____

____

____

How did it affect your relationship with your husband? How did it change your relationship with God?

____

____

____

____

David Brings Uriah Before Him

SCRIPTURE READINGS:

Day One: 1 John 1:3-4 (Try Not to Sin)

Day Two: Titus 1:16 (Denying God with Sin)

Day Three: Romans 2:8 (Do not Act Selfish)

Day Four: Exodus 23:21 (Obey God's Voice)

Day Five: Romans 2:23 (Dishonoring God)

Day Six: Psalm 107:17 (Afflicted by Foolishness)

Day Seven: 1 Timothy 1:9 (Laws Are Made for The Ungodly)

[6]"And David sent to Joab, saying, Send me Uriah the Hittite. And Joab sent Uriah to David.[7] And when Uriah was come unto him, David demanded of him how Joab did, and how the people did, and how the war prospered.[8] And David said to Uriah, Go down to thy house, and wash thy feet. And Uriah departed out of the king's house, and there followed him a mess of meat from the king.[9] But Uriah slept at the door of the king's house with all the servants of his lord, and went not down to his house." 2 Samuel 11:6-9

When David learned that Bathsheba was pregnant with his child, he came up with a plan to kill Bathsheba's husband Uriah in the war, so he wouldn't know that Bathsheba had betrayed him and had slept with someone else. This Bible passage details the first stage of his plan. He sent word to one of the people in his army, Joab, and told him to let Uriah return from the war. So, Joab sent word that Uriah was to return to the palace and have an audience with David.

When Uriah came before him, David casually started talking to him and asked him how Joab was and how the war was going. Then he urged Uriah to go down to his house and wash his feet. But instead of obeying the king's orders and returning to his home, Uriah left the palace and stayed outside, at the palace entrance that night with all of his master's servants. Plus, to make him think that David really favored him, David sent a gift to Uriah.

David wanted to kill Uriah because he and Bathsheba had slept together, and he knew both of them had betrayed Uriah. He had betrayed Uriah by sleeping with his wife and getting her pregnant. Bathsheba had betrayed her husband by having an affair while she was married to Uriah.

Even worse, she had an affair while her husband was off fighting a war that the guy she was sleeping with had launched against their enemies. Remember that Uriah was a soldier in David's army. He had gone to serve both David as his king and his wife, Bathsheba. He had gone to serve and protect his country and David's kingdom. But instead of sending someone to kill Uriah right away, David knew he had to do it in steps and that he had to do it discreetly.

David, at that time, is a cold person to want to kill someone's husband just so that the guy wouldn't find out about the affair and pregnancy. It is said in a later passage that Bathsheba knew of David's plan to kill her husband and urged him not to go through with his plan. They both knew that they had done wrong. Bathsheba most likely didn't want Uriah to find out that she had an affair with David. David wanted to eliminate any problems that would arise when Uriah found out that Bathsheba was pregnant because he knew Uriah would find out when he returned from the war.

DISCUSSION QUESTIONS:

Have you ever had an affair outside of your relationship or marriage? Did you and the guy try to hide it from your husband?

____

____

____

____

____

Did you become pregnant as a result of you cheating on your husband? What things did you do to hide your affair?

____

____

____

____

____

Did the guy you had an affair with ever start plotting against your husband? Did you go along with it?

____

____

____

____

____

JOURNAL QUESTIONS:

Did you ever have an affair while your husband was away fighting in a war? What did you do to cover up the affair?

____

____

____

____

____

How far were you and the other person willing to go to cover up the affair?

____

____

____

____

____

What does this lesson teach you about having affairs?

____

____

____

____

____

WEEK 23

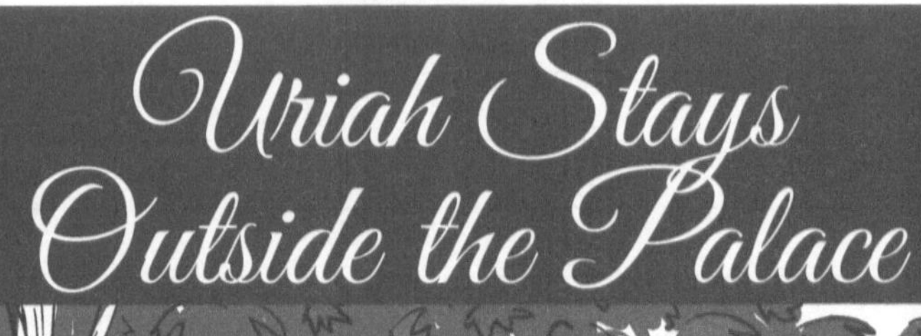

SCRIPTURE READINGS:

Day One: Romans 13:17 (Respect Others)

Day Two: Philippians 2:3-4 (Do Not Be Selfish)

Day Three: 1 Peter 2:17 (Honor Everyone)

Day Four: Leviticus 19:15 (Do No Injustices)

Day Five: Exodus 20:12 (Honor Your Parents)

Day Six: Ephesians 5:33 (Love Your Wife as Yourself)

Day Seven: Romans 13:1 (Be Subject to Governing Authorities)

¹⁰"And when they had told David, saying, Uriah went not down unto his house, David said unto Uriah, Camest thou not from thy journey? why then didst thou not go down unto thine house? ¹¹And Uriah said unto David, the ark, and Israel, and Judah, abide in tents; and my lord Joab, and the servants of my lord, are encamped in the open fields; shall I then go into mine house, to eat and to drink, and to lie with my wife? as thou livest, and as thy soul liveth, I will not do this thing.¹² And David said to Uriah, Tarry here to day also, and tomorrow I will let thee depart. So, Uriah abode in Jerusalem that day, and the morrow.¹³ And when David had called him, he did eat and drink before him; and he made him drunk: and at even he went out to lie on his bed with the servants of his lord, but went not down to his house."

2 Samuel 11:10-13

The next morning David found out from his army commander Joab that Uriah didn't go home. So, he sent for Uriah again and asked him why he didn't obey his orders to return home to his wife the night before. Uriah then told David that the ark of the covenant, Israel and Judah, were all staying in tents, so he felt he shouldn't go home to his wife. He wanted to honor the army and his commander by humbly staying outside of the palace. He even mentioned that David's army and his commander Joab were all camping in the open country. So, he didn't feel right about going home to see his wife Bathsheba and make love to her or eat, drink, and have a good time when everyone else was fighting in the middle of a war. He assured David that he would never do such a thing.

David then urged him to stay with him for two more nights. Uriah obeyed his orders this time and stayed in Jerusalem for two more days. David then sent for him again, and Uriah came to him. David had fun with him and got him drunk, thinking that drinking would get Uriah to go home to his wife and make love to her. However, David was wrong about Uriah. Even though he was drunk on David's wine, he still didn't go home to his wife. Instead, he went to sleep on the mat outside with his master's servants.

Uriah probably thought the king must have favored him to send for him three times to have an audience with him. Little did he know that David was plotting to kill him. David's first two plans were falling apart, so he came up with a new plan, as we will find in the next passage.

Women everywhere take this into account- if you ever have an affair and become pregnant with the other guy's child, your husband will eventually find out. Either before or after you have the baby. Do not go to the lengths that king David did to hide the affair and pregnancy from Uriah. Bathsheba knew about David's plans to kill her husband. You might wonder that since she had known about David's plans, what might she have done to stop him from going through with it? You might also wonder how David could go so wrong, from being a true man of God to plotting to commit murder.

What would you do if you found out the person, you'd had an affair with was plotting to kill your husband?

____

____

____

____

____

Would you try and stop it or do nothing?

____

____

____

____

____

____

What is your reaction to this story so far?

____

____

____

____

____

____

What are your thoughts on David going from being a man of God to committing murder because of his own mistake?

____

____

____

____

____

____

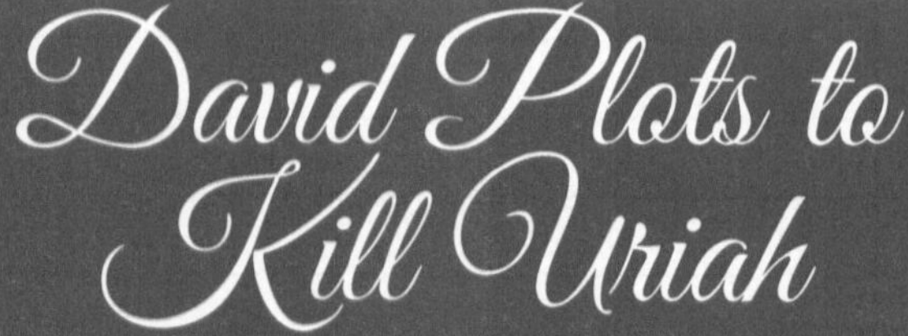

SCRIPTURE READINGS:

Day One: Leviticus 24:17 (Whoever Kills Will Be Put to Death)

Day Two: Mathew 5:21 (You Shall Not Murder)

Day Three: Romans 12:19 (Vengeance is God's Alone)

Day Four: Genesis 9:6 (Whoever Sheds Innocent Blood Will Perish)

Day Five: John 8:44 (Descriptions of Satan)

Day Six: Romans 6:23 (Wages of Sin Is Death)

Day Seven: Exodus 21:12 (Whoever Strikes A Man Will Be Killed)

[14] "And it came to pass in the morning, that David wrote a letter to Joab, and sent it by the hand of Uriah. [15] And he wrote in the letter, saying, Set ye Uriah in the forefront of the hottest battle, and retire ye from him, that he may be smitten, and die. [16] And it came to pass, when Joab observed the city, that he assigned Uriah unto a place where he knew that valiant men were. [17] And the men of the city went out, and fought with Joab: and there fell some of the people of the servants of David; and Uriah the Hittite died also." 2 Samuel 11:14-17

The last and most heinous part of David's plot comes in this passage. David sent a letter to the commander of his army, Joab. He told him to put Uriah at the front of the battle that was happening, where the fighting was the most dangerous just so he would get killed. He even told his commander to get away from Uriah and not offer him any help in the middle of the battle. Joab knew he couldn't and shouldn't refuse any of the king's orders, so he did exactly as David told him. This passage then goes into detail about what Joab did and where he placed Uriah. It tells you that Joab had the city put under siege, and he had Uriah placed at the forefront of the fighting so he would be killed. During the battle, many of David's men died. So did Uriah.

Who knows what David felt when he got word that Uriah had been killed in the battle? He must have been feeling a wide range of emotions. Those emotions could have ranged from shock and awe and probably for the smallest amount of time; maybe David was even feeling a bit of relief. He might have been feeling shocked and awe and relieved that his plan had actually worked. He might have been feeling guilty for having another man killed just because he had had an affair with his wife and that he had gotten Bathsheba pregnant. He could have been feeling guilty because he was usually a man of righteousness and a man of God, not to mention a man of integrity and honor. He knew that God had seen him sin, and he knew that God knew he was going to sin, even before he had Uriah killed.

What emotions had Bathsheba felt after she had heard of her husband's death in war? It says later in the chapter that she was heartbroken that Uriah was dead. You might wonder what else she might have been feeling? Maybe, in the back of her mind, she felt relief that no one else on Earth besides she and David would know about the pregnancy. After all, she had come to and slept with the king that was anointed by God! She was now the mother of his child. She might have been shocked that David would stoop so low as to kill Uriah. You can learn a lot from this passage. Just because you want to do something doesn't mean that you should go through with it.

DISCUSSION QUESTIONS:

What is your reaction to hearing that David actually went as far as to have Uriah killed just to cover up his own mistake?

Would you ever be with someone who was plotting against your husband's life?

What would your reaction be if you were Bathsheba and found out that your husband died in the war? Would you ask questions or let it go?

What would you do if you were David? Would you ever be happy if you received news that a person was killed because you'd ordered it?

____

____

____

____

____

What would you have done if you were Bathsheba and had just lost your husband?

____

____

____

____

____

WEEK 25

SCRIPTURE READINGS:

Day One: 1 John 1:9 (Confess Sins and Be Cleansed from Unrighteousness)

Day Two: James 5:16 (Confess Sins and Pray With One Another)

Day Three: Psalm 32:5 (Acknowledge Sins to Others)

Day Four: Proverbs 28:13 (Confess Sins to Obtain Mercy)

Day Five: 1 Timothy 2:5 (Mediator of All Is God)

Day Six: John 20:23 (Forgiveness is Either Given or Withheld)

Day Seven: Romans 3:23 (All Have Sinned)

[13] "And David said unto Nathan, I have sinned against the Lord. And Nathan said unto David, The Lord also hath put away thy sin; thou shalt not die.[14] Howbeit, because by this deed thou hast given great occasion to the enemies of the Lord to blaspheme, the child also that is born unto thee shall surely die.[15] And Nathan departed unto his house. And the Lord struck the child that Uriah's wife bare unto David, and it was very sick.[16] David therefore besought God for the child; and David fasted, and went in, and lay all night upon the earth." 2nd Samuel 12:13-16

This isn't where David's and Bathsheba's love story transformed into them living happily ever after, just like in a fairy tale. On the contrary, actually. Here is a bit of a back story: The opposite of a fairy tale came upon them because of both their sins. The Lord's servant Nathan came to David and told him that he knew he had killed Uriah so he wouldn't find out about David's and Bathsheba's affair. But he did it cleverly. Nathan told David the story about two men in a certain town. One was rich, and one was poor. The rich man had everything from cattle to sheep, but the poor man had nothing except a little lamb that he and his family had cared for.

The man and his family had loved that little lamb with all their hearts and had treated it like it was a member of their family. Then a traveler came to the town where the men lived. The rich men refused to make a meal for the traveler. However, the man who loved the lamb took it and prepared it for the traveler so he could eat. You read that correctly. The poor man was willing to sacrifice the lamb he loved so the traveler could eat, but the rich man made no such sacrifice. David was furious and said that whoever had the lamb killed should have to die and give the person who sacrificed the lamb four more lambs. Nathan then admitted that it was David who was that man. Nathan then told him what the Lord said about his plan to kill Uriah in secret and then told him that God's punishment for David would be in front of Israel for everyone to see. David would lose his wives and his splendor as a king.

David finally admitted that he had sinned against the Lord by having Uriah killed. Nathan assured him that he wouldn't die because of his sin and that the Lord forgave him. However, the baby that David had helped Bathsheba produce was then born, and their son eventually became very sick and died. David pleaded with God for the child's life to be spared, and he fasted all night. No doubt that David was utterly heartbroken that his son was dying and that there was nothing he could do to save him. If only he hadn't plotted to kill Uriah, the child would have still been alive and thriving. But because of his own selfish desires, he cost his own son his life. Bathsheba was probably heartbroken, too, at the loss of her son.

DISCUSSION QUESTIONS:

What would your reaction be if you were in David's shoes and a messenger of the Lord came to you telling you that your son would die because of your plot?

____

____

____

____

____

____

What would you do if you were told that your newborn son would get sick and die because of your mistake? Would you instantly be filled with re-morse and regret?

____

____

____

____

____

____

How would you try and save your child's life from being taken away from him because of your mistake?

____

____

____

____

____

____

Would you fast the way David did and plead to God through prayer for your child's life to be spared?

____

____

____

____

____

____

WEEK 26

King Solomon's Wives

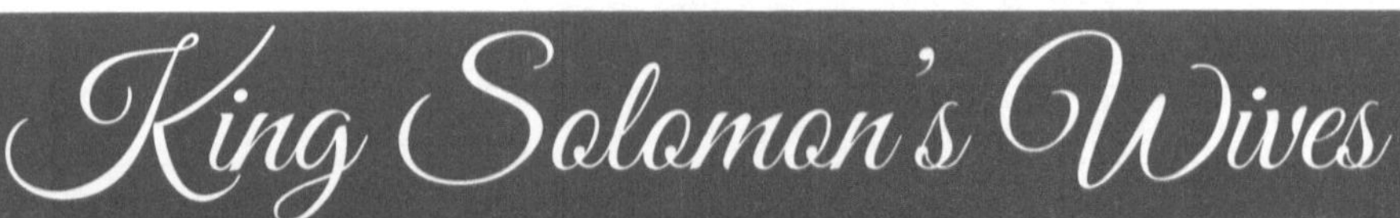

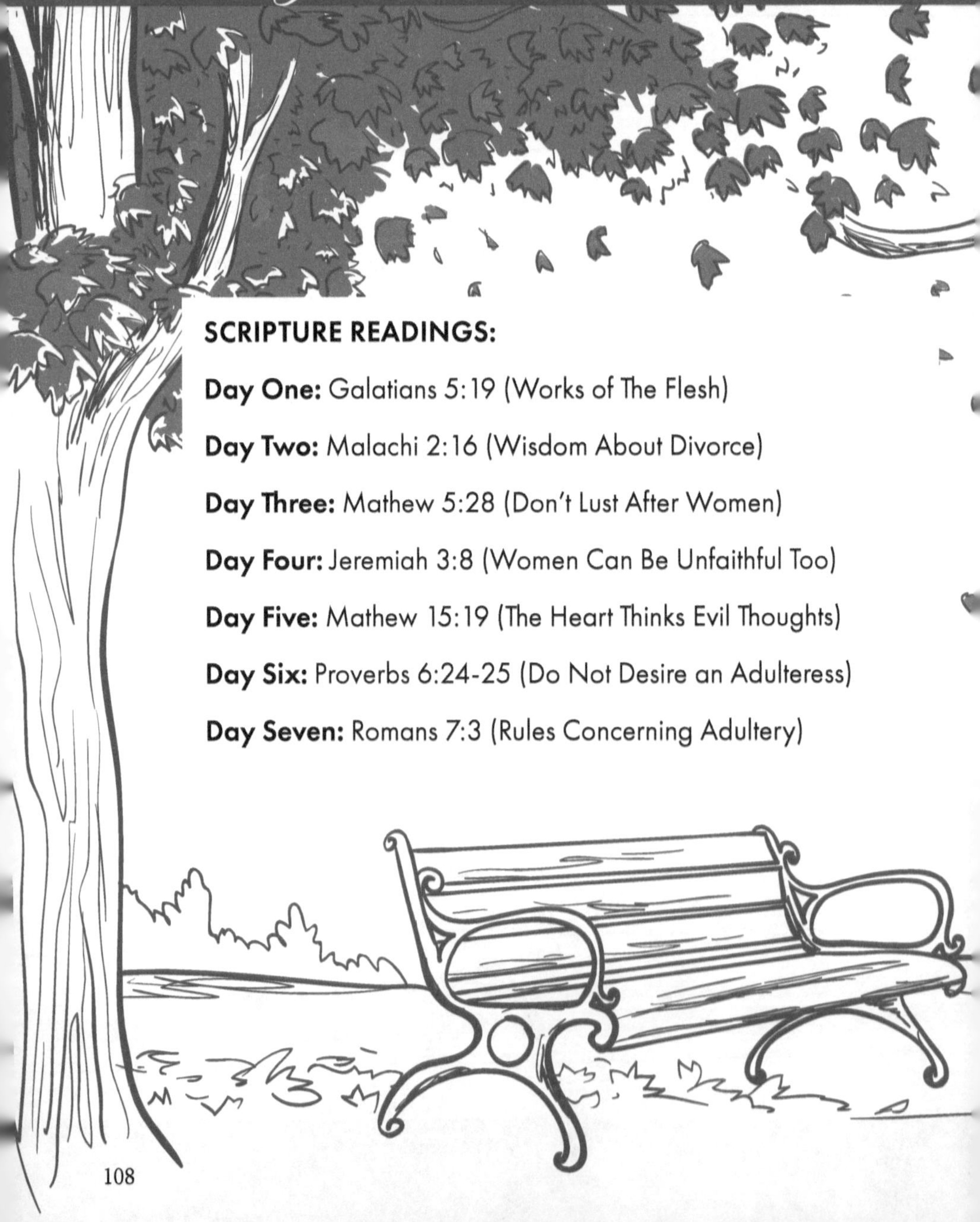

SCRIPTURE READINGS:

Day One: Galatians 5:19 (Works of The Flesh)

Day Two: Malachi 2:16 (Wisdom About Divorce)

Day Three: Mathew 5:28 (Don't Lust After Women)

Day Four: Jeremiah 3:8 (Women Can Be Unfaithful Too)

Day Five: Mathew 15:19 (The Heart Thinks Evil Thoughts)

Day Six: Proverbs 6:24-25 (Do Not Desire an Adulteress)

Day Seven: Romans 7:3 (Rules Concerning Adultery)

[1] "King Solomon, however, loved many foreign women besides Pharaoh's daughter—Moabites, Ammonites, Edomites, Sidonians and Hittites. [2] They were from nations about which the Lord had told the Israelites, "You must not intermarry with them, because they will surely turn your hearts after their gods." Nevertheless, Solomon held fast to them in love. [3] He had seven hundred wives of royal birth and three hundred concubines, and his wives led him astray. [4] As Solomon grew old, his wives turned his heart after other gods, and his heart was not fully devoted to the Lord his God, as the heart of David his father had been." 1 Kings 11: 1-4

King Solomon was one of the wisest people in the Bible. He, however, had a downfall. He loved many different women, from Pharaoh's daughter to Moabite women, Ammonite women, Edomite women, Sidonians women, and even Hittite women. The Lord gave a stark warning to the Israelites that they were not supposed to marry any of these women because He knew they believed in other gods. The Lord also knew that they would turn the Israelites away from Him and manipulate whoever married them to start worshiping their gods instead of worshiping Him as the one true God, the one who delivered them from slavery in Egypt.

King Solomon disobeyed God and His warning about those women and fell madly in love with them. As crazy as it sounds, the Bible actually tells us that he had 700 wives. You might be wondering, "how can anyone man have that many wives in his life? How did he keep track of that many women? What does he do with them all day, every day? The Bible doesn't tell us what he did with them all the time or how he kept track of them, but it does tell you that he had 700 wives of royal birth, as well as 300 concubines and that all of those women lead him astray in his life. His heart was not fully devoted to God as David was, which caused him to be led astray by so many women.

The moral of this story is: women do your best to not lead anybody astray, especially your husbands. Always make sure they are in tune with God and protect their personal relationships with God every day. There are several ways in which you can do that. You can pray for them and with them when they start and end their day. You can read the Bible with them every day.

You can also ask them what they need prayers for in their daily life and do your best to always pray for their specific needs. Their needs can change from week to week, given their stress level and their jobs. If they seem stressed out more than usual, then you can calmly ask them what is wrong and remind them that God is always there for them even in times when they think He is entirely absent from their lives. Always make sure you both are going to church every week. If you make worshiping God a habit, your marriage will only get stronger, and you will be able to face many more trials together.

What other things can you do to lead your husband in the right direction with his faith?

____

____

____

____

____

How can you help him want to learn more about God every day?

____

____

____

____

____

How can you both keep God as the top priority of your lives and in your marriage?

____

____

____

____

____

What can you learn from this Bible passage about keeping God at the center of your marriage?

____

____

____

____

____

Where do you notice that you and your husband are going astray in your relationship with God?

____

____

____

____

____

Are you leading each other down the path of righteousness?

____

____

____

____

____

WEEK 27

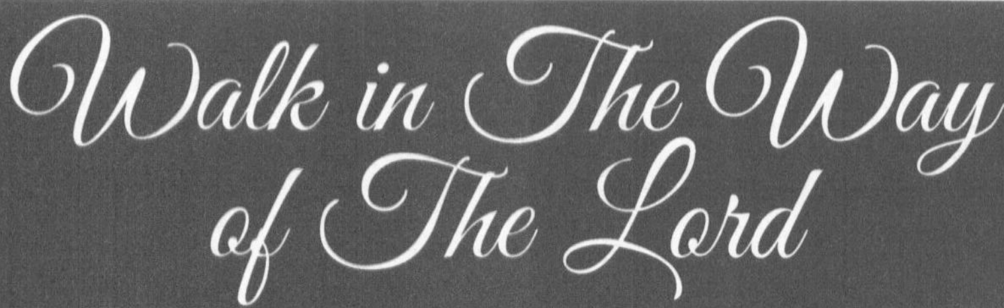

SCRIPTURE READINGS:

Day One: Proverbs 22:6 (Train A Child in The Way He Should Go)

Day Two: Deuteronomy 6:5-9 (Repeat God's Word to You Kids)

Day Three: Mathew 19:13-15 (Let the Little Children Come to God)

Day Four: 1 Timothy 4:10-11 (Teach Everyone About God)

Day Five: Deuteronomy 11:19 (Talk About God with Your Children)

Day Six: Proverbs 23:13-14 (Discipline Your Kids)

Day Seven: Proverbs 22:15 (Discipline Protects Your Kids)

"And keep the charge of the Lord thy God, to walk in his ways, to keep his statutes, and his commandments, and his judgments, and his testimonies, as it is written in the law of Moses, that thou mayest prosper in all that thou doest, and whithersoever thou turnest thyself: 4 That the Lord may continue his word which he spake concerning me, saying, If thy children take heed to their way, to walk before me in truth with all their heart and with all their soul, there shall not fail thee (said he) a man on the throne of Israel." 1 Kings 2:3-4

This Bible passage tells women to always observe what the Lord requires of them. Walk in close connection and obedience to Him every day. Keep His decrees and His commands, as well as His laws and regulations as they were written in the Bible. Keeping His commands makes you honorable in His sight. Whenever you keep His commandments, you aren't sinning, and you feel better every time you do the right thing. Do this so you may prosper in everything you do in your life, as well as where ever you may go in your life. Let the Lord lead your life in everything that you do.

If you keep His commandments every day, the Lord will keep His promises to bless you in your life. Teaching your children about God and how much a relationship with Him can and will change their lives is the best thing you can do for your kids. It is more important than any education in a school or any other relationship that they will ever have with a boyfriend or girlfriend.

If your descendants and children watch how you live your life, they will live by your example. All you have to do is teach them about who God is and how He can change their lives and impact their life for the better. You can teach them how to pursue God with everything they have and how they can have a deep personal relationship with Him in each of their lives.

If they can stop themselves from sinning as much as they can every day, then they will know that if they at least try their hardest, God smiles on them. He knows that they will sin every day, but you can teach your children that even though they sin daily, they can still approach God and ask for His forgiveness with all their heart. If your children watch how they live their lives and do their best to please God every day, they will go far in their lives.

If you teach your children to be faithful and walk faithfully before God every day of their lives, you are helping them change their lives for the best. A relationship with God and eternal salvation is the best gift you can ever give your children on Earth and in their heavenly life. If they do their best to know God on a deeply personal level in everything they do early in life, they will know how to respond to difficult situations better later in life.

What have you taught your children in their walk with the Lord? What are their favorite things about God? What are their favorite Bible verses?

____

____

____

____

____

What have you noticed in their faith walk? How have they been living out their faith in everyday situations?

____

____

____

____

____

As they've grown, have you noticed a shift in their faith walk, or has it stayed the same?

____

____

____

____

____

What are your favorite things to teach your children about God?

____

____

____

____

____

What has been the hardest thing to teach your children about God?

____

____

____

____

____

What has been the easiest/simplest thing to teach your children about God's love?

____

____

____

____

____

SCRIPTURE READINGS:

Day One: Jeremiah 29:11 (God knows His plans For Your Life)

Day Two: Romans 8:28 (All Things Work Together for Good)

Day Three: Psalm 33:11 (The Plans of The Lord Stand Firm)

Day Four: Jeremiah 1:5 (God Knew You Before You Were Born)

Day Five: Psalm 32:8 (God Will Teach You Where to Go)

Day Six: Proverbs 3:5-6 (Trust God Through Everything)

Day Seven: Philippians 4:13 (You Can Do All Things)

¹³"Then Mordecai commanded to answer Esther, Think not with thyself that thou shalt escape in the king's house, more than all the Jews.¹⁴ For if thou altogether holdest thy peace at this time, then shall there enlargement and deliverance arise to the Jews from another place; but thou and thy father's house shall be destroyed: and who knoweth whether thou art come to the kingdom for such a time as this?"
Esther 4:13-14

Esther was a young girl who had become queen after King Xerces found favor with her. After being the queen of all Persia for a while, she learned of a terrible plot against her and her family by the king's henchman and right-hand man Haman. Haman was quite evil and hated Mordecai, who Esther was related to. He plotted to kill Mordecai after he had saved the king's life because he was jealous of Mordecai.

When Esther learned that she, Mordecai, and her entire family, including all Jews, would be killed by Haman, she wasn't sure what she could do. Mordecai was trying to convince her to go to the king and inform Haman's plan. Esther was afraid for her life and her family's life, and she knew how evil Haman was. She also knew that no one was supposed to go before the king without having been invited by him first. Anyone that went before him without being invited by him first was going to be punished by death. She expressed her fears to Mordecai. He reassured her that there was no other way to save their family.

He told Esther that perhaps she was put in her position of power as the queen for that particular time and that she was put in that position just to save her family and all of the Jews. Esther finally agreed to go before the king after much thought and prayer, not to mention many prayers from Mordecai and her entire family. Esther was afraid for her and her family's life, and she had every reason to be afraid of requesting an audience in front of the king, even though she was in a position of power as the queen. She knew she could get killed if she asked for an audience with the king, especially if she appeared before the king unannounced.

This story can teach you that instead of thinking that you don't have a purpose in your life or thinking that you won't do anything in life, look at where you are in your life. You are placed in the very position that you're in for God's specific purpose. He knows why you are in your particular situation and how you will impact His kingdom. Wherever you are in your life, think of ways you can impact God's kingdom in your home, work-life, among your friends, and around your family. You could just save someone's life.

DISCUSSION QUESTIONS:

In what ways can you help impact God's kingdom the way Esther did?

How can you overcome your fears of making someone aware of the bad things that may be happening in your life or your workplace?

Who can you talk to that is in a position of power about the situation, just like Esther was told to approach the king?

How can you overcome your fears of telling others about God and his goodness in your life?

JOURNAL QUESTIONS:

How can you work through your fears of ever speaking out against the injustices you see in your workplace, home life, and even any injustices you may see among your family and friends?

____

____

____

____

____

What things can you do to make people in authority aware of the situation? Have you prayed for the courage to act?

____

____

____

____

____

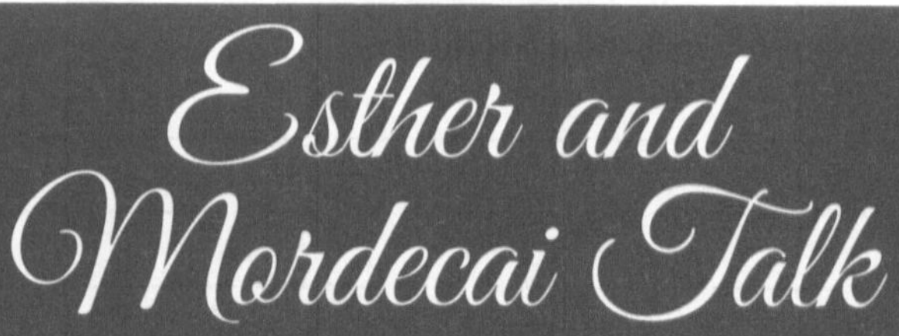

Esther and Mordecai Talk

SCRIPTURE READINGS:

Day One: Ephesians 2:10 (We Are His Workmanship)

Day Two: Mathew 6:16-18 (Rules for Fasting)

Day Three: Isiah 58:3-7 (Humble Fasting)

Day Four: Joel 2:12 (Return to God)

Day Five: Psalm 69:10 (Fasting as a Reproach)

Day Six: Daniel 10:3 (How Long You Can Fast For)

Day Seven: 1 Corinthians 7:5 (Don't Deprive One Another)

¹⁵ Then Esther bade them return Mordecai this answer,¹⁶ Go, gather together all the Jews that are present in Shushan, and fast ye for me, and neither eat nor drink three days, night or day: I also and my maidens will fast likewise; and so, will I go in unto the king, which is not according to the law: and if I perish, I perish. ¹⁷ So Mordecai went his way and did according to all that Esther had commanded him."
Esther 4:15-17

This story continues with Esther telling Mordecai to request all of the Jews in Shushan to fast with her. She requested that he tell the Jews not to eat or drink anything for three days. Esther and her maidservants would fast too. She was planning on going to the king, even though it was against the law to appear before the king without him requesting an audience when the fasting was over. She started having a bit of courage ending with this statement: "If I perish, I perish." That means that she was ready to go to the king even if it meant losing her life to tell him about Haman's evil plot against her, her family, and the rest of the Jews. She knew she could be killed, but she knew she had to take that chance to save her family and her people.

Esther was very heroic, and she realized that maybe she was placed in her position of power as the queen for that exact moment, to have the power and authority to save her family and all of the Jews. Think about it, if she was still a peasant girl, then she wouldn't have been able to get anywhere near the king or ever been able to talk to him.

All women everywhere can take this story and put it in their hearts. If Esther was ready and willing to go to the king to tell him about Haman's evil plot against her family, then you surely can speak out against any injustices and evil you see in your life, whether it's a personal struggle with your family, a work struggle, or anything in between. If Esther could risk her life to save her family, you can also make others aware of what is happening in your life.

There is nothing wrong with making the right people aware of what things are happening in your life. If something is happening in your family that you know is wrong, speak out, tell someone about it, no matter what happens to you because of it. Pray for courage and the strength to speak out. Ask that God would give you the right words at the right time when you are put in front of the right people, with God's power in His timing. He will help you know what to do and what to say in any of those situations. You just might end up saving someone's life by speaking out against any injustices that you see.

Does this passage give you the courage to speak out and let people know that you're not afraid of stepping up for your coworkers, friends, or family?

____

____

____

____

____

In what areas can you start having the courage to speak out about things in your life?

____

____

____

____

____

What areas of your life do you need others to pray for you how Esther re-quested Mordecai and her family pray for her?

____

____

____

____

____

In what areas have you requested prayers from people in your life?

____

____

____

____

In what ways does this passage give you the courage and strength to speak out where you need to speak out?

____

____

____

____

Have you prayed for the courage to bring awareness to things that need to be known?

____

____

____

____

Have you ever had the courage to risk your own life to save your family's life?

____

WEEK 30

Esther Tells King Xerces Haman's Evil Plot

SCRIPTURE READINGS:

Day One: Proverbs 6:12-16 (The Lord Detests Wicked People)

Day Two: Ecclesiastes 12:14 (Every Deed Is Brought Before God)

Day Three: Psalm 34:21 (Affliction Will Slay Wicked People)

Day Four: Micah 2:1 (Woe to The Wicked)

Day Five: Psalm 37:1 (Don't Be Envious of Evildoers)

Day Six: Romans 3:10 (No One Is Righteous)

Day Seven: 1 Thessalonians 5:22 (Abstain from Every Form of Evil)

[3] "Then Esther the queen answered and said, If I have found favor in thy sight, O king, and if it please the king, let my life be given me at my petition, and my people at my request: [4] For we are sold, I and my people, to be destroyed, to be slain, and to perish. But if we had been sold for bondmen and bondwomen, I had held my tongue, although the enemy could not countervail the king's damage. [5] Then the king Ahasuerus answered and said unto Esther the queen, who is he, and where is he, that durst presume in his heart to do so? [6] And Esther said, the adversary and enemy is this wicked Haman. Then Haman was afraid before the king and the queen." Esther 7: 3-7

So, Esther invited Haman and the king to three different banquets before she was completely ready to tell the king of Haman's evil plot. At the third banquet, as they were all drinking wine, Esther was preparing for her big moment, all the while knowing that once she told the king of Haman's plot, she could end up dying herself. As they were drinking wine, the king asked Esther again what her request was. He then told her he would give her up to half of his kingdom if she requested it. That's an extremely generous thing to offer, whether you're a king or not, but especially for him to offer it to Esther. After all, she hadn't been queen for that long.

Esther then probably took a deep breath and then proceeded to tell the king what was on her mind. She probably said a silent prayer and then proceeded to tell him the truth. She said if it pleased the king and that if she had found favor in his eyes, she requested that the king spare her life as well as the life of all the Jews and the rest of her family.

She then explained to the king that she and her people, the Jews, had been sold to be killed. She continued to explain her circumstances, saying that if she and her family had just been sold as slaves, then she would have kept silent because no distress would have been worth disturbing the king. The king must have been both shocked and in horrible awe hearing what Esther said. He then asked Esther where the man was who would do such an evil thing and asked who he was. She then turned to the king and told him that it was Haman, his right-hand man.

Once the king knew that Haman was plotting against him, Esther, and her entire family, and the entire Jewish population, he was outraged. The king then left in a rage. Haman knew his fate was sealed and that the king was going to kill him, so he stayed behind and begged Esther to spare his life.

Think of it this way, if Esther hadn't been brave enough to speak up and try to save her family, so many people would have been killed. Who knows what else would have happened besides God Himself? Let this story inspire women everywhere to have the courage to speak out against anything that they know is wrong in their lives.

In what areas of your life can you take courage and talk about the injustices you see?

____

____

____

____

What areas of your life are you nervous to tell others about?

____

____

____

____

Have you prayed for the courage to be able to tell someone what may be happening in your personal life, work-life, or with your friends? Who can you talk to?

____

____

____

____

In what areas of your life can you assume the courage of Esther?

____

____

____

____

____

In what areas of your life can you pray for courage?

____

____

____

____

____

How has God revealed to you how to approach someone in authority?

____

____

____

____

____

WEEK 31

Job's Trials

SCRIPTURE READINGS:

Day One: Job 2:1-7 (Job's Test)

Day Two: Job 2:8-9 (Job's Wife's Plea)

Day Three: 1 Peter 5:10 (God Will Establish You)

Day Four: Romans 8:18 (Glory Is Coming)

Day Five: James 1:2-4 (Faith Produces Perseverance)

Day Six: Psalm 34:19 (God Delivers the Righteous)

Day Seven: 2 Timothy 3:12 (Living Godly Lives)

[9] "Then said his wife unto him, Dost thou still retain thine integrity? curse God, and die.[10] But he said unto her, Thou speakest as one of the foolish women speaketh. What? Shall we receive good at the hand of God, and shall we not receive evil? In all this did not Job sin with his lips." Job 2:9-10.

In this Bible passage, Job is a very faithful man of God. He is so faithful to God that he doesn't stop praising God even when he has the most difficult times of his life. He lost his children, family and was being attacked by the world and by Satan at every turn. God and Satan actually had a one-on-one conversation where Satan wondered who else he could torment and torture. God actually offers up Job so he could be tested by Satan fully. God actually said, "Have you considered my servant Job?" God told Satan he could test Job to his limits but couldn't physically lay a hand on him.

God probably willingly gave Job up to be tortured mentally, emotionally, and physically by Satan because He knew that Job wouldn't ever forsake Him as his Lord and Savior. Satan probably thought: "wow, God is actually letting me torture someone that believes in Him. I have the inside track because God is letting me do these horrible things to Job. He won't want to worship God after I get through with him. I will make him forget how good God is and make him only see misery for all of his days. No one will want to worship God after what I do to Job."

Surprisingly, the person that wanted Job to stop professing his faith in God was his own wife! She actually told him that it would be better to curse God and die than for Job to live in misery. However, Job refused to turn away from God because he knew God was the only reason he was getting through the most difficult times. He knew that God was still good and was still with him despite the pain he was going through. He knew there was nothing he couldn't get through with God at his side.

He actually told his wife that she was acting like a foolish person asking him to curse God and die. Then he asked her, "should we only receive good from God and not trouble?" That meant that he asked her whether we should just expect that we should only be happy in life and not suffer in our lives. Without the hard times, we wouldn't know how to lean on God and ask Him to guide us through the rough waters. Without pain, there would be no reward. Without pain, we wouldn't appreciate the good times or the blessings in our lives.

DISCUSSION QUESTIONS:

What difficult times have you gone through in your life? How have you clung to God and His strength during those times?

____

____

____

____

____

What have you done to stay close to God instead of turning away from Him?

____

____

____

____

____

Have you ever had someone try to convince you to turn away from God because of the pain you were going through in your life?

____

____

____

____

____

Have you ever thought about turning your life away from God because of the things you were going through? How did He help you realize that He was and is always with you?

____

____

____

____

What is the hardest thing you've ever gone through in your life? How did God help you get through it?

____

____

____

____

____

How did you cling to God even when you felt like giving up on Him and His plan for your life?

____

____

____

____

____

What did you learn through this story about Job? How can you assume some of Job's faith in your circumstances?

____

____

____

____

____

WEEK 32

SCRIPTURE READINGS:

Day One: Psalm 37:4 (Delight in The Lord)

Day Two: Psalm 1:1-6 (Walk with The Lord)

Day Three: Psalm 16:8 (Never Shaken)

Day Four: Psalm 51:10 (Clean Heart)

Day Five: Psalm 119:33-40 (Ask for Understanding)

Day Six: Proverbs 29:25 (Safe in The Lord)

Day Seven: Nehemiah 8:10 (Joy of The Lord)

"Blessed is the man that walketh not in the counsel of the ungodly, nor standeth in the way of sinners, nor sitteth in the seat of the scornful.[2] But his delight is in the law of the Lord; and in his law doth he meditate day and night. And he shall be like a tree planted by the rivers of water, that bringeth forth his fruit in his season; his leaf also shall not wither; and whatsoever he doeth shall prosper." Psalm 1:1-3

This Bible passage tells you that you should be very careful who you're around daily. If your crowd of family, friends, or anyone in your inner circle is starting to act wicked towards God, you, or anyone else, you need to get out of that circle no matter how hard it may be for you. It also tells you not to walk in the same path that sinners of the world take and to not be in the company of mockers. That might get you thinking, "How can I not live in sin? I'm not perfect. I know that God knows I'm not perfect, but I'm trying my best to not give in to the temptation of walking with, hanging out with, or being influenced by the wrong crowd in my life. If I'm hanging with the wrong crowd and those people happen to be in my family or my friends' circle, how do I get away from their negative influence? How do I not let them influence me? How do I walk away from them when they need to know Jesus?"

You can still help them get to know God in their life by praying for them and, if you're able to, praying with them. You can always tell them how Jesus has impacted your life for the better. If they're curious about how to obtain salvation, that is your perfect time to share the good news of the Gospel with them. You can tell them how they can lay their sinful nature at the foot of the cross as you do every day. You can tell them that you aren't perfect but that God loves you just like He loves them, no matter what they may have done.

It says, in this passage, anyone who doesn't walk in the ways of the wicked or take the same path sinners to take will be blessed and rewarded by God. Blessed are those who take delight in the law of the Lord and who meditate on His law every day and night. So as much as you can, take notice of who you're hanging out with and change your habits around them. Keep your focus on God no matter where you are, no matter who you're with, and be a reflection of Jesus in everything you say and do. You could impact someone's life for the better. You could end up saving someone's life. Never give up on sharing the good news of Jesus in everything you do. Be His example.

In what ways can you walk in righteousness and be Jesus' example in everything you say and do?

____

____

____

____

In what ways has God told you to get out of the wicked crowd you may hang out with?

____

____

____

____

How can you take the straight and narrow path instead of taking the path that fits in with the crowd of the world?

____

____

____

____

What can you do to show the goodness of God in your life every day?

____

____

____

____

____

Where can you point the people in your life to Jesus?

____

____

____

____

____

In what ways have you had to make hard choices to walk away from wicked people, protect yourself physically, mentally, emotionally, and most importantly, protect yourself spiritually?

____

____

____

____

____

WEEK 33

Virtuous Women

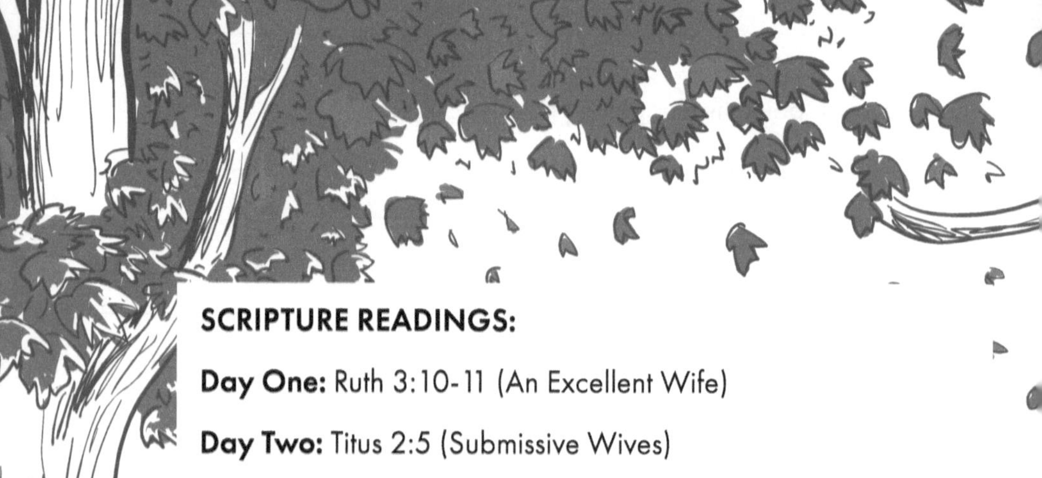

SCRIPTURE READINGS:

Day One: Ruth 3:10-11 (An Excellent Wife)

Day Two: Titus 2:5 (Submissive Wives)

Day Three: Proverbs 31:27 (Smart Women)

Day Four: Ruth 3:1 (Naomi and Ruth's Discussion)

Day Five: 1 Peter 3:1-6 (Obey Your Husbands)

Day Six: 1 Corinthians 7:2-5 (Do Not deprive One Another)

Day Seven: 1 Peter 3:7 (Honor Your Wife)

Are you a wife of noble character? Do you honor your husband and God every day of your life? Don't worry. God knows that every person on Earth sins every day. All He wants you to do is be the person He made you be in your life. Whether it's a wife, mother, daughter, niece, granddaughter, sister, or even the CEO of a company, God just wants you to do your best at whatever you do each day.

A noblewoman is a crown to her husband, but any wife that makes her husband ashamed is a disgrace to him and God. This passage says that a disgraceful wife is like decay to her husband's bones. You might be thinking that this verse is a little too harsh for your liking. There is nothing wrong with thinking that thought. All God says in this passage is that He wants you to be honorable towards your husband, which means submitting to what he asks of you as long as what he is asking you is within your reasoning and beliefs.

As long as what he is asking is within your beliefs, you can willingly do what he asks you. It doesn't mean submitting to him if he does something physically or mentally, or even emotionally abusive to you. If your husband does any of those things, you need to ask God for His guidance and for Him to give you the courage to get out of that situation no matter what it takes.

If there is something that needs to be discussed, calmly approach your husband about it. Ask God for the right words to start the conversation. Ask God to be with you through the entire conversation and for you to not get angry even if your husband doesn't agree with the things that you're bringing up. Ask God to help you come to a truce and to end each conversation with love. If you can learn to approach your husband with love and honor him, you can be a much better wife.

This verse means that you should always do your best to honor your husband and make him happy. Keep your eyes focused on God and keep Him at the center of your relationship and at the forefront of your marriage. If you do those things, your relationship will prosper and be blessed beyond what you could ever ask or fathom. There is nothing you both can't get through with God at your side.

In what ways can you change yourself to become a better wife each and every day? What areas of your marriage do you know you need to invite God back into?

____

____

____

____

____

What can you do to bless your husband, even if it's only through a small loving gesture such as making a meal for him?

____

____

____

____

Have you asked God to guide you in your interaction with your husband daily? How can you show love to your husband if he is going through a difficult time at work or with his family?

____

____

____

____

____

In what ways can you be a wife of noble character, as this verse states?

____

____

____

____

How has God spoken to you through this passage? What have you learned through this passage about being a good wife to your husband?

____

____

____

____

____

How can you change your attitude, tone of voice, and even change your body language to be a better wife to your husband every day?

____

____

____

____

____

What different ways do you try to be a better person and a better wife every day?

____

____

____

____

____

WEEK 34

SCRIPTURE READINGS:

Day One: Ecclesiastes 5:4-6 (Do Not Delay Your Vow)

Day Two: Deuteronomy 23:21-23 (Vows in Front of God)

Day Three: James 5:12 (Don't Swear by Heaven)

Day Four: Numbers 3:20 (Bound to A Vow)

Day Five: Psalm 61:8 (Sing Praises)

Day Six: Job 22:27 (Prayers)

Day Seven: Mathew 5:33-37 (Don't Swear Falsely)

When you make a vow, do your best to fulfill it for God. That means if you tell God to use you in ways that only He can use you to better His kingdom, then do not back down on that promise that you made to Him. Just go out and be His light and His example in your life, in your interactions and love every person. If you promise to be a witness to people in your life, whether you know them or not, then be His witness. The Lord takes no pleasure in fools, but He delights in those who know His truth and who keep their word.

That also means that if you promise a friend or family member, do your best to fulfill that promise. If you make a promise to someone to go to their house for dinner, then go to their house. If you promise your daughter one on one time despite your busy work schedule, then spend time with her, because before you know it, she will be grown up and have her own life. If you made your elderly mom a promise to make her cookies for the holidays or to visit during the holidays, then not only should you fulfill that wish, your entire family should go and visit her if they can.

If you made a promise to your family member that you would help them clean their house, then honor that commitment and clean their house with them. If you promise your boyfriend that you're going to go on a date, then go on a date with him. Do not say to someone that you will do something and then turn around and not do it. Everyone gets annoyed when someone in their lives says that they will do something with them, and then the person doesn't follow through with their obligations.

When you don't keep your word, it also disappoints God. God wants you to keep your word to everyone that you make promises to. Every time you make a promise to a friend, your boyfriend, or your husband or family member, just do it. Don't get cold feet or be scared to do it. Remember, the time you spend with others means a lot to them. It means a lot to God too. It's better to keep your promises to people than to make promises and not fulfill them. If you don't want to do something for someone, then never make that promise in the first place.

In what ways can you always keep your commitments to people, even if you're afraid to keep them?

____

____

____

____

____

How can you honor the vows you took in front of God to be a witness for Him for the better of His kingdom?

____

____

____

____

____

Have you asked God to help you honor the commitments you made to your friends, family, boyfriend or husband, extended family, or even your boss?

____

____

____

____

____

How can you honor your commitments to people even if you have second thoughts about going through with them?

____

____

____

____

____

What makes you second guess going through with the commitments? Is it the fear of forgetting about your commitments altogether, the fear of rejection, the fear that something will go wrong, or some other fear that you have?

____

____

____

____

____

How can you turn all of those nervous feelings over to God? Do you trust that He is with you through any circumstance that makes you anxious?

____

____

____

____

____

Loving Kindness of God

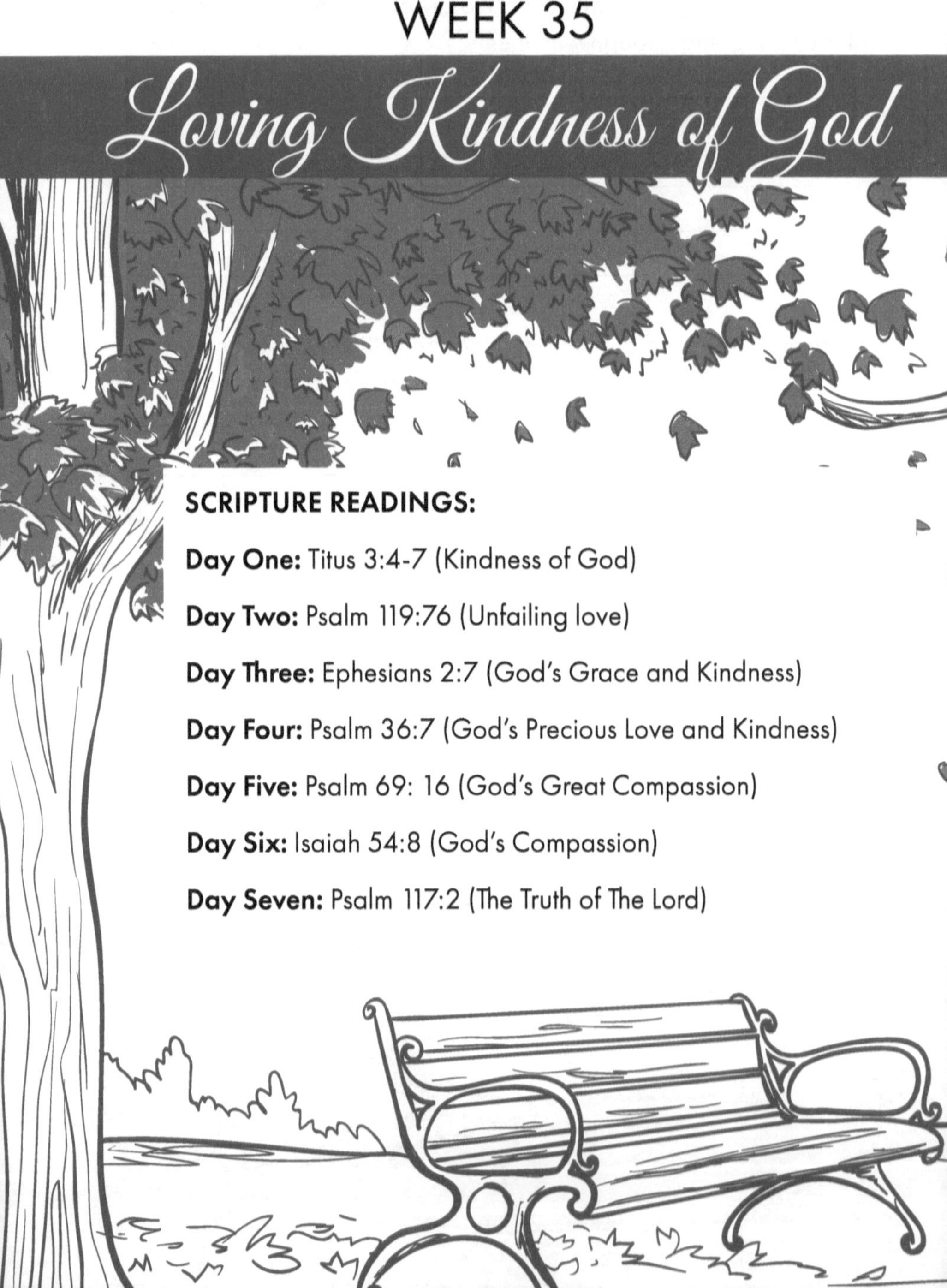

SCRIPTURE READINGS:

Day One: Titus 3:4-7 (Kindness of God)

Day Two: Psalm 119:76 (Unfailing love)

Day Three: Ephesians 2:7 (God's Grace and Kindness)

Day Four: Psalm 36:7 (God's Precious Love and Kindness)

Day Five: Psalm 69: 16 (God's Great Compassion)

Day Six: Isaiah 54:8 (God's Compassion)

Day Seven: Psalm 117:2 (The Truth of The Lord)

"I will mention the loving kindnesses of the LORD, *and* the praises of the LORD, according to all that the LORD hath bestowed on us, and the great goodness toward the house of Israel, which he hath bestowed on them according to his mercies, and according to the multitude of his loving kindnesses." Isaiah 63:7.

The Lord never stops showing His kindness to people in their lives. Think back to when He showed kindness and love to you, your friends, or your family members. When the Israelites were enslaved in Egypt, God promised them that He would bring them a deliverer to save them from their slavery. Little did they know that it would be Moses who would get them out of Egypt by the power of God and help them make it across the Red Sea on dry land, only to have them watch as God swept the Egyptians away in the Red Sea. At the time, they didn't know that Moses wouldn't make it into the Promised Land and that God would appoint someone new named Joshua to lead them into the Promise Land.

God also gave them mana to eat and enough water to drink when they walked in the wilderness for forty years. Despite all of their complaining and grumbling, God still was with them. They eventually started praising Him again with thankfulness in their hearts. You can also thank God for the great things He has done for you. He gives you food and drinks every day. You've never gone thirsty or hungry. You have a home to rest peacefully in every night. You have so many different ways to relax every day after you get home from work. You have a job that helps you provide for your family. Your kids are doing well in school and in life. God is protecting you and your family from harm physically, mentally, emotionally, and even spiritually. You have true Godly friends and a family that is willing to do anything for you at a moment's notice, no matter what the circumstances may be. You are blessed more than you realize. Take the time to notice all of the blessings that He has given you in your life. God is always with you, no matter what happens in your life. He never abandoned the Israelites, and He will never abandon you in your life. You will never have to figure out life on your own because He is only a prayer away. Declare the goodness of God over your life and in every situation. If you can learn to praise Him no matter what may be going on and give thanks for everything you have, you will live a much calmer, healthier, and happier life. Start praising Him every day and see how your life changes for the better.

DISCUSSION QUESTIONS:

How have you mentioned the Lord's kindness to your friends, co-workers, or family members? How has God been gracious and kind to you in your life?

____

____

____

____

____

How have you given Him the praise and thanks He deserves?

____

____

____

____

____

____

What amazing things has He done for you in your life? How has worshiping Him and giving Him thanks changed your life?

____

____

____

____

____

How have you mentioned the Lord's loving-kindness to people in your life? What has that experience of being a witness for Him been like for you?

____

____

____

____

____

How has the Lord's kindness and love changed your life for the better? Have you seen changed behavior in your friends or family since you started declaring how good God really is?

____

____

____

____

____

Have you noticed changes in your mindset since you started giving God praise every day?

____

____

____

____

WEEK 36

SCRIPTURE READINGS:

Day One: Proverbs 3:5-6 (Lean Not on Your Own Understanding)

Day Two: Psalm 9:10 (Those Who Know God)

Day Three: Psalm 28:7 (God Is Your Strength)

Day Four: Psalm 46:10 (God Will Be Exalted)

Day Five: Romans 15:13 (Abound in Hope)

Day Six: Mathew 6:25 (Be Anxious for Nothing)

Day Seven: Psalm 112:7 (Firm Hearts)

"Blessed is the man that trusteth in the Lord, and whose hope the Lord is.[8] For he shall be as a tree planted by the waters, and that spreadeth out her roots by the river, and shall not see when heat cometh, but her leaf shall be green; and shall not be careful in the year of drought, neither shall cease from yielding fruit."
Jeremiah 17:7-8

You will be blessed in your life if you keep your eyes on God. God sees those who are devoted to Him, and He will reward those faithful to Him. If you keep your confidence in God even in the middle of hard times, you will learn to see the blessings even in the middle of the hard times. You will start to see beauty where there used to be no beauty. You will start being grateful for the things you have in your life instead of being annoyed at how things are going in your life. You will start being grateful for things instead of whining and complaining that you don't have the things you want.

If you keep your focus on God as much as you can in your life, this passage says that you will be like a tree planted by the water, where the roots can easily get nutrients from the water. It doesn't fear when the heat comes because its leaves are always green. It also doesn't worry if there is a drought, and it never fails to bear fruit.

If you keep yourself close to God by reading His word every day, you will learn more about Him and actually want to learn more about Him. You'll actually crave fellowship and alone time with Him every day. If you keep close to God, you will succeed in your life. Yes, you will have struggles and trials, but you will be able to get through them a heck of a lot easier with Him in your life than what you would be able to get through them without Him. If you try to get through things without Him, you will become more confused, frustrated, and fed up as each day goes on. But if you know God, you will be able to think clearly through difficult situations and make much better decisions. You won't worry about your life. You will be centered and focused. If you get nutrients and knowledge about how to live and love God's word, you will know how to react and how not to react to people in life. When you know God, you won't fear hard times in your life as much. You will be ready to face them with God at your side, and you will know that you will be able to count on Him way more than you could ever count on anyone else in your life.

DISCUSSION QUESTIONS:

In what ways can you keep your focus on God? In what ways can you remind yourself that God is always with you, even during your hard times?

____

____

____

____

____

How has God gotten you through hard times in your life? In what ways has
God showed His power in your life?

____

____

____

____

____

How have you been like a tree planted by the water in your faith walk?

____

____

____

____

____

JOURNAL QUESTIONS:

How has God helped you not to lose sight of Him in your life? How has He blessed your life?

____

____

____

____

What has God revealed to you during your faith walk?

____

____

____

____

What is your favorite thing that you've learned about God through your journey?

____

____

____

____

What was the hardest thing you've had to learn in your faith walk so far?

____

____

____

WEEK 37

SCRIPTURE READINGS:

Day One: Psalm 18:2 (God Is Our Strength)

Day Two: Psalm 62:6 (Stronghold)

Day Three: Psalm 46:1-3 (God Is Your Refuge and Strength)

Day Four: 2 Samuel 22:31 (God's Way Is Perfect)

Day Five: Psalm 5:11 (Sing for Joy)

Day Six: Psalm 7:1 (Save Me from Pursuers)

Day Seven: 1 Peter 5:8 (Watch Out for Satan)

The Lord is the only person strong enough, brave enough, and caring enough to carry all of your sins on His shoulders at any time. Whether it's day or night, He will hear you whenever you cry out to Him. He loves every one of His children equally, and He wants to know you on a deeply personal level. Whenever you go through hard times, you often forget that He is with you because you're so focused on the dark cloud looming over your head and over your life. Satan fills your heart with dread, and he makes you forget that you can always call on the Lord no matter what you may be feeling.

Satan can start messing with your mind when he makes you think that you're not qualified to do a certain task or have a certain position. He gets under your skin and makes you feel inferior, and he doesn't have a chance to succeed in the new position. Satan can make you feel as though you're unworthy and that God didn't even call you or qualify you for the position that you're trying to get, or he can even make you feel under-qualified as a wife, mom, daughter, granddaughter, niece, aunt, sister or as a friend. He can make you doubt yourself as you try to climb the cooperate ladder.

This Bible passage says that the Lord is a stronghold for you to cling to during any day that starts giving you trouble. If you can turn your focus away from the feeling of defeat and onto the power that God has given you, you will be able to get through any obstacle that comes your way. You will be able to focus on the tasks that are in front of you clearly. You will be able to confidently approach every task and every assignment. Instead of dreading each day and wanting it to be over, you can have a calm mindset and a ready heart to tackle each day.

Even when you start feeling as though you can't go on, and when Satan makes you feel like giving up for different reasons, God will give you the strength that you didn't even know that you had within you. He knows you and loves you, and He wants you to succeed in everything you do. As long as you have trust and faith in Him, He will help you do the things He has put before you.

DISCUSSION QUESTIONS:

What things do you dread at your work every week? What things at home give you anxiety?

____

____

____

____

____

How can you turn from your worries and refocus on the One who can get you through each of those worries?

____

____

____

____

____

What areas of your life are you struggling to keep the faith?

____

____

____

____

____

How can you remind yourself not to give in to the despair that Satan tries to cloud your mind with?

____

____

____

____

____

How can you enjoy every moment of your life instead of dreading every moment? What did you learn from this Bible verse?

____

____

____

____

____

What can you help teach others about the Lord as a stronghold over your life? How can you be an inspiration and speak positive affirmations not just over your own life, but to speak positive affirmations to other people and over their lives when they need encouragement too? When you see someone needing encouragement, what things can you say to them about God's love?

____

____

____

____

____

What have you done to be Jesus' light and His example when you notice someone going through dark times? How have you resisted Satan's attacks in your daily life? What has God revealed to you when Satan attacks you in different ways?

____

WEEK 38

SCRIPTURE READINGS:

Day One: Isaiah 1:19 (Be Willing and Obedient)

Day Two: Hebrews 13:17 (Submit to Your Leaders)

Day Three: Romans 6:16 (Obedience Leads to Righteousness)

Day Four: James 4:7 (Submit Yourself to God)

Day Five: John 14:21 (Love God)

Day Six: Luke 11:28 (Hear God's Word)

Day Seven: 2 Corinthians 10:5 (Destroying Arguments)

³⁵ "And the angel answered and said unto her, The Holy Ghost shall come upon thee, and the power of the Highest shall overshadow thee: therefore, also that holy thing which shall be born of thee shall be called the Son of God.³⁸ And Mary said, Behold the handmaid of the Lord; be it unto me according to thy word. And the angel departed from her." Luke 1:35-38

This passage gives women everywhere a great idea of just how amazing and powerful God is. Here, Mary was told that she had found favor with God and that she would be the mother of Jesus, who was to be the Savior of the entire world. Understandably so, Mary was frightened at the sight of the angel and even more frightened and shocked by his announcement. She even asked him, "how can I have a child if I've never been with a man and I'm still a virgin?" When the angel of the Lord announced that she would be pregnant by the Holy Spirit and that the child would be God's one and only son, Mary must have been in complete shock.

But, the most amazing thing happens after the angel tells her all of these jaw-dropping details about her life and her future. Mary boldly comes before God and the angel of the Lord, saying, "I'm your servant Lord. Let all of this be done unto me according to your word." After she'd made this declaration of obedience before God Himself, the angel left her.

In today's day and age, not very many women would boldly approach God and say, "ok Lord, let it be done unto me." Most women nowadays would be extremely timid and afraid if an angel appeared to them telling them that kind of amazing news. This passage teaches you to boldly come before God and tell Him that you're allowing Him to do whatever He wants to do in your life. It also teaches you about the kind of faith that Mary had in God. It teaches you the love and even the level of respect that Mary had for God. Mary had the type of faith and obedience that would make her a force to be reckoned with. Mary had found much favor in the Lord's sight, so she knew she had to listen to what the angel of the Lord was saying to her.

She knew that she couldn't tell the angel, "no, you've got the wrong girl. This can't happen to me." She loved God and had complete trust and faith in Him, even before the angel answered her questions of "how can this be?" Mary respected and believed what the angel of the Lord was saying to her. Then she willingly surrendered her entire life in obedience to the Lord's beautiful and divine plan. Little did she know that she would be impacting the entire world.

DISCUSSION QUESTIONS:

How would you feel if an angel of the Lord appeared to you and told you that you would give birth to the Savior of the world?

____

____

____

____

What would you say to him? Would you willingly accept the task he gave you, or would you be unsure of accepting the assignment he gave you?

____

____

____

____

How would you handle such a big task as being the mother of the Savior? Would you feel qualified and up to the task, or would you feel afraid of what God was telling you?

____

____

____

____

What did you learn from this passage? How can you summon up the courage like Mary did when she was told that she had found favor with God and would be the mother of Jesus?

____

____

____

____

____

____

In what areas of your life has God called you to your higher purpose, just as He called Mary to her purpose?

____

____

____

____

____

____

WEEK 39

SCRIPTURE READINGS:

Day One: 1 John 1:6-10 (Truth Isn't in Us)

Day Two: 1 John 1:9 (Cleansed from Unrighteousness)

Day Three: Romans 5:8 (Christ Died for Us)

Day Four: John 3:16 (God Loved the World)

Day Five: James 1:27 (Pure Religion)

Day Six: Philippians 2:9 (God Is Highly Exalted)

Day Seven: Ephesians 1:4 (Holy and Blameless Before God)

8 "If we say that we have no sin, we deceive ourselves, and the truth is not in us. 9 If we confess our sins, he is faithful and just to forgive us our sins and to cleanse us from all unrighteousness. 10 If we say that we have not sinned, we make him a liar, and his word is not in us." 1 John 1:8-10

Everyone has fallen short of the mark and has sinned against God. Every woman in history has made mistakes and sinned against her fellow women and against her family and friends. It is even worse to deceive yourself and think that you don't sin or think that you don't have any sin within your mind, body, soul, and heart. This Bible passage says if you say you have no sin, you deceive yourself and the truth is not even in you. That's a harsh statement to hear from God about yourself.

It even goes on to say that if you say that you haven't sinned and denied that you sin every day, you actually make God a liar. You might be thinking, "wait, how can I make God a liar?" If you openly say that you didn't sin, even though you know deep in your heart and deep in your sub-conscience that you were wrong, you're not only lying to yourself, you're also lying to God. Remember, God sees, hears, and knows all. He knows everything about you before you were even born into existence. He knows your thoughts before you even speak a thought into existence. He knows how you're going to sin every day, down to the smallest detail of the sin that you commit.

Remember that sinking feeling that you get each and every time you tell someone a lie? That is the Holy Spirit telling you that you shouldn't have lied and that you should have just told the truth. Telling the truth doesn't give you that same sick feeling in the pit of your stomach that lying does.

If you deny yourself that you sinned, you also deny it before God because God is all present and all-knowing. There's no point in denying that you've sinned because God already knows that you sinned. However, if you confess your sin and wrongdoing before God, He will willingly forgive you and cleanse you from all of your sin and unrighteousness.

This passage tells you that God knows everything about you. He knows that you will make mistakes and sin. Instead of telling you that to scare you, God then tells you that if you willingly ask for forgiveness with all of your heart, He will cleanse you from all of your sin and unrighteousness. This Bible passage tries to steer all women in the right direction.

Have you ever said that you were without fault for a mistake you made even though you sin every day? How have you tried to turn the guilt that you were feeling onto someone else?

____

____

____

____

____

Did Satan ever make you think that sinning wasn't really sinning? How did God change that mindset around to help you realize that you were only fooling yourself into thinking you hadn't sinned?

____

____

____

____

____

In what ways have you realized that the truth of God isn't always in you?

____

____

____

____

____

JOURNAL QUESTIONS:

Have you ever unintentionally made God out to be a liar? In what ways has Satan tricked you into thinking that you hadn't sinned when you really had sinned?

____

____

____

____

____

How did you make God out to be a liar when you thought you didn't sin against Him?

____

____

____

____

____

How did God return you to the right path? How did God help you come before Him and ask for His forgiveness?

____

____

____

____

WEEK 40

No One Is Righteous

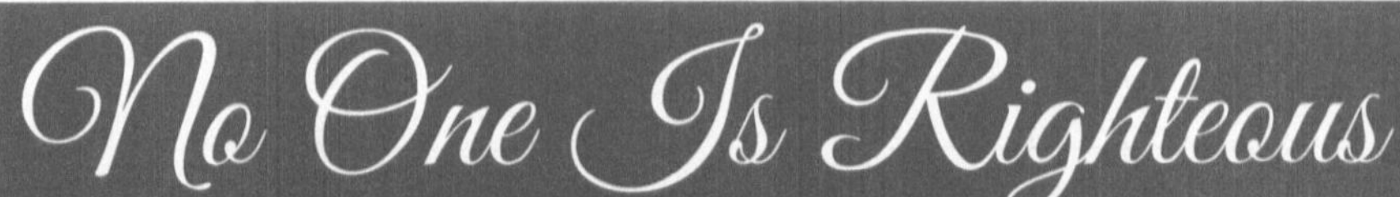

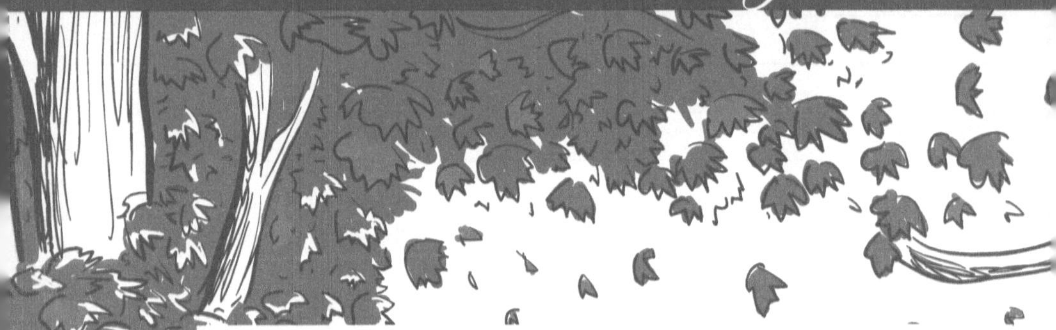

SCRIPTURE READINGS:

Day One: Numbers 23:19 (God Will Not Change His Mind)

Day Two: Ephesians 4:22-23 (Put Off Your Old Self)

Day Three: 2 Corinthians 6:14 (Don't Be Unequally Yoked)

Day Four: 2 Corinthians 5:17 (New Creation in Christ)

Day Five: Acts 16:31 (Believe in God)

Day Six: John 1:12 (Children of God)

Day Seven: 2 Corinthians 3:6 (The Spirit Gives Life)

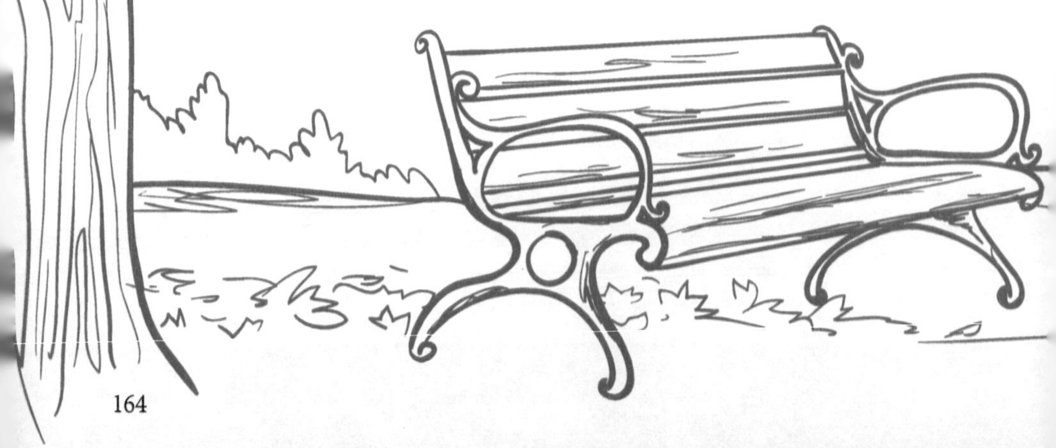

"As it is written, There is none righteous, no, not one:[11] There is none that understan-
deth, there is none that seeketh after God.[12] They are all gone out of the way, they
are together become unprofitable; there is none that doeth good, no, not one."
Romans 3:10-12

Not one person, man or woman, is righteous in their life. Not one. Think about that for a second. There is not one person on Earth who really understands Jesus. The only person who truly understands Him is God. This passage also tells you that no one truly seeks God with all their heart, soul, and mind. No one really seeks Him in the way they were meant to or how they were originally supposed to seek Him before the first sin was committed. No one takes the time to really listen to what God is trying to tell them in the way that they're supposed to. No one gets to know God on a deep and personal level how they would get to know Him before the first sin was committed.

 Before the first sin was committed, everything was literally perfect on earth. Everything was in perfect harmony, and everything that God made was good. Adam and Eve obeyed and worshiped God before the first sin. They had one on one time with Him whenever they wanted to. They walked with Him in the Garden of Eden.

After the first sin, everything and everybody were corrupted by Satan and his sick mind games and deception. Now thanks to Satan, no one is ever going to be seen as righteous or good in the eyes of God. Every person has turned away from God instead of turning towards Him and getting to know Him on a deeply personal level.

This passage goes on to explain that everyone has become worthless. You might think that it might be pretty harsh to have God say that about you or anyone. But it's true. No one is considered sinless, good, or righteous in God's eyes except Jesus because Jesus is the only one who didn't sin in His life. The only way to become worthy in God's eyes is to admit your sinful ways, confess them before God, and try not to sin again.

Even though you'll fail, God knows that you're trying your best to do good in your life. He wants you to try to be like Jesus in everything you say and do. This means being kind to unkind people, being silent in the middle of heated discussions when they may not involve you, and standing up for people who can't stand up for themselves. It also means spreading the good news of Jesus to everyone around you, no matter how they may treat you.

How have you tried seeking God in everything that you do in your life? Have you ever considered yourself to be more righteous and more of a Christian than other people around you?

____

____

____

____

____

If you ever thought that, in what ways did you think that you were better than other people? In your work ethic, your family or church life, or even in your relationship with God?

____

____

____

____

____

What did you learn from this passage? What can you teach others about this passage?

____

____

____

____

____

What areas of your life can you be humbler before both God and before your fellow man? Where can you improve your self-righteous attitude?

How can God help you improve your attitude about your life? What areas of your life have you realized are unprofitable? Your mindset and attitude, your interactions with people at work or at home?

What about the quality time you spend with God? How do you change your attitude from being self-righteous to have a humbler attitude?

WEEK 41

Knowledge of God

SCRIPTURE READINGS:

Day One: Proverbs 18:15 (Intelligent Heart)

Day Two: Proverbs 1:7 (Fear of The Lord)

Day Three: Proverbs 15:14 (Seek Knowledge)

Day Four: Proverbs 24:5 (Be A Woman of Knowledge)

Day Five: 1 Corinthians 1:8 (Love Builds Up)

Day Six: Colossians 2:3 (Hidden Treasures of Wisdom and Knowledge)

Day Seven: Ecclesiastes 7:12 (Wisdom Preserves Life)

"That in everything ye are enriched by him, in all utterance, and in all
knowledge;[6] Even as the testimony of Christ was confirmed in you: [7] So that ye
come behind in no gift; waiting for the coming of our Lord Jesus Christ."
1 Corinthians 1:4-7.

The way you approach everything and everyone in your life is important.
It's important to remember that God has given you many unique abilities and talents. He has given you abilities that no one else has, and He
has a specific purpose in mind for your life. It is your job to discover what that
purpose is and to learn something new every day in the process. Think about
what your divine purpose is in your life and think about what kind of calling
He placed on your heart. Maybe you're supposed to be a teacher or a principal.
Maybe you're supposed to be the manager or CEO of a company. Maybe you're
supposed to be a stay-at-home mom, so you can spend every precious moment
with your kids instead of working. Maybe you're supposed to help the needy in
your community by volunteering at a charity.

Whenever you start thinking that you may not measure up in the workforce or
in your home life, remember, God didn't just think you "might be able to do the
job" or that you "might be good as a mom or a caregiver." No, God knew where
He needed to place you at the exact moment that you're in right now. He has
you in whatever position you're in for His reason. He called you to your position because He knew that you would be good at it already.

He has never doubted your abilities, so don't doubt yourself. God knows exactly how, why, and where you are supposed to use your abilities. He will help you
learn how to use them in the best way possible. Remember, God doesn't waste
anything. He can use you to impact His kingdom.

By God's grace, you are enriched by Him every day. You have the right words to
say at the right time. You have the right abilities that God will help you use at
His timing. You have the knowledge from God that you can use at any time, day
or night, to get yourself through any situation.

If you ever feel stuck, you can ask God for guidance, and He will give it to you.
Jesus Christ is among you and within you, in your spirit. This passage reveals
to you that you don't lack any spiritual gift from God as you wait for the second
coming of Christ. From the time you were born until you go to Heaven, He has
placed His Holy Spirit within you. Use the gifts He's given you for His glory.

DISCUSSION QUESTIONS:

What do you think your God-given abilities are? How can you use them for His glory and purpose?

____

____

____

____

____

If you're still searching for your God-given abilities, how have you approached God and asked Him to reveal His plan for your life?

____

____

____

____

____

Do you ever compare your abilities to someone else's and think that you don't measure up in the same way? Do you ever doubt yourself or think that your abilities don't matter?

____

____

____

____

____

What is your favorite God-given talent that He gave you? What is the hardest one for you to use? Why is it the hardest one to use?

____

____

____

____

____

How do you use your God-given talents every day and in every situation? What is one gift that God gave you that you get to use, where you just look up to Heaven and say, "God, I know that this gift came from you"?

____

____

____

____

____

How long did it take you to discover what your unique talents are? How has God helped you use them?

____

____

____

____

____

WEEK 42

SCRIPTURE READINGS:

Day One: James 1:13-18 (Resist Temptation)

Day Two: Luke 22:40 (Pray to Resist Temptation)

Day Three: Mathew 6:13 (Deliver Us from Temptation)

Day Four: Luke 11:4 (Forgive Those Who Sin)

Day Five: 1 Corinthians 10:13 (Enduring Temptation)

Day Six: 1 Peter 4:12 (Tests of The World)

Day Seven: 2 Peter 2:9 (Unrighteous Punishment)

If you've ever been caught in the middle of sin, you know how it feels to get caught red-handed. You probably felt guilty and wanted to apologize for it. That feeling in the pit of your stomach is almost enough to make you sick. If you've ever felt that nudge of the Holy Spirit letting you know that you could be making a serious blunder if you choose to sin, that is God's way of getting your attention before you actually commit the sin. He offers you guidance as to what is right and what is wrong.

God also gives you the free will to choose whatever you want to do. It is your choice to realize that you're wrong and ask God for forgiveness and ask Him to help you to not sin anymore. It is also your choice to ignore the sins you committed and act as if they're not a big deal.

If you've ever caught someone else that was about to sin, what did you do to try to help them not to sin? You might be wondering, "how can I actually help a person who is sinning or help a person who is about to sin?" Here are some things that you can do: You can pray for them to see the error of their ways. If God moves you to help them see the errors of their ways, then ask Him how and when you should approach them. He will give you the right words to say at the right time. When it's the right time, ask them if they have time to talk to you for a bit.

Even before you're talking to them, ask God to give you the courage to speak about the person's sin in a way that they can understand it. Help them understand that they did something wrong without having an accusing tone in their voice. Point out their sin and explain to them calmly why it was wrong and how they can correct it.

Explain to them that God offers them the free will to choose what they want to do. Explain that God offers them forgiveness as long as they ask for forgiveness and mean that they are truly sorry. Let them know that they need to apologize to whoever they committed the sin against, not just to God. Once they ask for forgiveness, tell them to try not to sin anymore. Do your best to not get caught up in their sinful ways and guard your heart.

Have you ever caught someone in sin? What did you do about it? How did you approach the person and talk to them about the sin they committed?

____

____

____

____

____

How did the person react when confronted about their sin? Did they deny it or try to cover it up?

____

____

____

____

____

How did God help you approach them gently, even if it was a big deal? How do you protect yourself by not getting caught up in the ways the person sins? What does this person say or do?

____

____

____

____

____

JOURNAL QUESTIONS:

How do you approach someone that you know who has committed a sin? What was your reaction to them sinning?

____

____

____

How do you protect yourself from sinning along with that person? How has God gotten your attention about the particular sins that this person may be committing?

____

____

____

____

How has He impressed upon your heart to not go down that same path? What things did you do to help that person turn away from their sin?

____

____

____

____

Have you seen any change in behavior with the person you have talked to since you talked to them about their sin?

____

WEEK 43

Glory of Jesus

SCRIPTURE READINGS:

Day One: Romans 15:17 (Boast About God)

Day Two: Philippians 4:19 (God Will Supply All Needs)

Day Three: Colossians 1:27 (Riches of Glory)

Day Four: Galatians 6:14 (Boast About the Cross)

Day Five: 1 Corinthians 1:31 (Boast in The Lord)

Day Six: Romans 11:36 (In Him Are All Things)

Day Seven: Colossians 3:4 (Revealed to You in Glory)

[20] "Now unto him that is able to do exceedingly abundantly above all that we ask or think, according to the power that worketh in us. [21] Unto him be glory in the church by Christ Jesus throughout all ages, world without end. Amen."
Ephesians 3:20-21

Whenever you feel as though you can't walk another step or can't go on another day because of the stress in your life, do you automatically turn to God, or do you stay in the same spot wallowing in your pain, misery, and sorrow, or even in your anger? Or do you turn things over to God and say, "Lord, I know you have this situation under control. Please help me to be calm and to think rationally and clearly through this problem."

God is the God of the universe. That means that He is able to do so much more than we could ever ask, think, or fathom in our minds. Remember, God is God. He knows and sees all things. Whenever you go through a hard time in your life, don't be afraid to go to God automatically and pray for His peace that surpasses all human understanding. Don't be afraid to go to Him and ask Him to restore all of the things you have lost. Maybe it's your marriage that needs restoring or strengthening, or your relationship with your friend, or your relationship with your boss at work. Maybe your health needs restoring, or you need a new job to come your way.

There is nothing too complicated for God to work on or work through. He can do immeasurably more than you could ever ask, think, or imagine in your life. His power is at work within you right now at this very moment. His power is always at work within you, even when you don't think He is at work in your life or that He is absent from your life.

He can restore your job, your relationship, your friendships, and your marriage. Anywhere you need help, you can call on Him, and He will answer you in His timing and His way.

Even in the middle of your hard times, you can still give praise to Him and thank Him for the wonderful things He has done in your life. You can give Him the glory and remember how He has gotten you through the tough times.

He has the power to restore anything you may have lost, and He can help you figure out how to get through any and all of those circumstances. If you can learn to give Him the glory even in your hard times, you can get through them with clarity and peace in your heart, knowing that He is with you every step of the way.

DISCUSSION QUESTIONS:

What hard times have you been going through in your life? What areas of
your life do you need to be restored?

____

____

____

____

____

Have you asked God for His peace through any difficult times you go
through? How has God given you peace and reminded you that He is always with you?

____

____

____

____

____

How have you reminded yourself to stop wallowing in your pity party and
come to God no matter what you're facing?

____

____

____

____

____

What has God restored in your life? How has He restored the things that you thought were beyond repair?

____

____

____

____

____

How has He redeemed your relationships with your friends and your marriage? How have you been able to give God thanks, glory, and praise even amongst the confusing and chaotic times in your life?

____

____

____

____

____

Have you been able to turn to God more every day, despite your circumstances? What has He revealed to you in your darkest moments?

____

____

____

____

____

WEEK 44

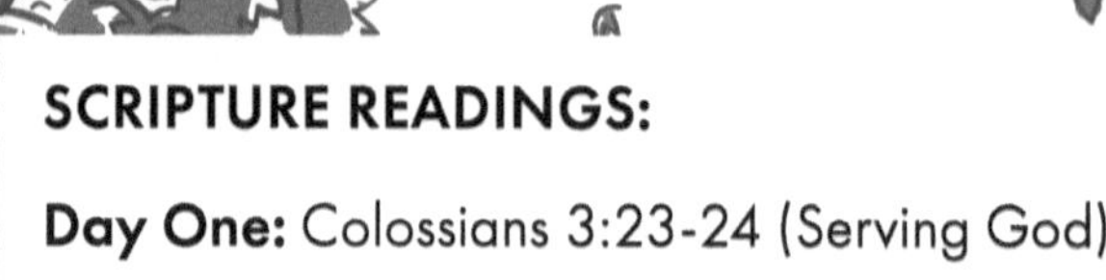

SCRIPTURE READINGS:

Day One: Colossians 3:23-24 (Serving God)

Day Two: 1 Corinthians 10:31 (Eat and Drink for God)

Day Three: 1 Corinthians 6:20 (Glorify God in Your Body)

Day Four: Mathew 5:16 (Let Your Light Shine)

Day Five: Romans 11:36 (All Things Are Through Him)

Day Six: Psalm 34:4 (Magnify the Lord)

Day Seven: Psalm 50:15 (God's Deliverance)

"And whatsoever ye do in word or deed, do all in the name of the Lord Jesus, giving thanks to God and the Father by him." Colossians 3:17

Whatever you do, whether you're thinking about something, or attempting to do something, remember who you're doing it for. Work at your job, your marriage, your relationship with your kids and your friends, and even at your hobbies as if you're doing it for the glory of God. He sees everything at all times and knows what you're going to do before you even do anything.

Even though it can be hard to remember to do everything as if you're doing it for the Lord, it is important to have that thought in your heart as often as possible. If you think about how your actions and reactions toward someone can affect them, then you're taking into account how everything you do has an equal and opposite reaction.

You're also taking into account how your reactions and your actions can make someone else feel. If you do something that makes someone second guess themselves or makes you second guess yourself, then you're doing it for the wrong reasons. If your reactions toward a friend make them shut down instead of open up to you more, ask God to guide you in ways you can repair that friendship. If all you think about is how the things you do affect you, you forget that your actions can affect other people.

If you're doing something for the good or only for the benefit it will bring you, you're struggling with the wrong mindset. So many times, you can get caught up and think about how you can reap the rewards when you do something right instead of trying to please God in the things you do. For example, let's say you're given a huge project at work with a promotion tied to the back end of it if you do a good job on the project. If you know everything can and will hang in the balance if you don't do well, you'll do everything within your power to do the project correctly.

The same thing goes for your relationship with God. Everything can and will hang in the balance if you don't work at everything in your life as if you're working for Him. The reality is that you are working for Him every day of your life and in every situation, whether you realize it or not. If you can start acting as if everything you do matters, you will go through life that much easier once you work at everything as if you're working for God. Give thanks to God for everything you do.

What do you do daily to glorify God? How do you glorify God in every-thing that you say and do?

____

____

____

____

____

Whenever you get caught up in the mindset of "how can this benefit me," how can you ask God to remind you that it is better to please Him with your words and actions than to get gratification for yourself?

____

____

____

____

____

How did God help change your mindset from only thinking about benefiting yourself to thinking of ways to glorify Him?

____

____

____

____

____

JOURNAL QUESTIONS:

Why is it sometimes so hard to honor God in everything you say and do? How can you change your mindset to actually want to honor God in everything you say and do, whether it's your work, school assignments, friendships, or relationships?

____

____

____

____

____

How can you remind yourself that it is better to please God in everything you do than please yourself?

____

____

____

____

____

Where can you go to escape the busyness and fast-paced life and to get closer to Him in everything you do? How can you remind yourself to give thanks to Him no matter what may be going on in your life?

____

____

____

Mystery of Godliness

SCRIPTURE READINGS:

Day One: 1 Timothy 1:5 (Only One God)

Day Two: John 1:14 (Word Became Flesh)

Day Three: Ephesians 1:20-23 (Fullness of God)

Day Four: Hebrews 7:25 (Draw Near to God)

Day Five: Romans 12:5 (One body To Christ)

Day Six: Isiah 7:14 (Give You A Sign)

Day Seven: Galatians 4:4 (Wonderful Counselor)

"And without controversy great is the mystery of godliness: God was manifest in the flesh, justified in the Spirit, seen of angels, preached unto the Gentiles, believed on in the world, received up into glory." 1 Timothy 3:16

This passage is kind of interesting as it points out Jesus and the mystery of true godliness. Many people have wondered at the greatness of Jesus and at the mystery of what it takes to achieve true godliness in their lives. This passage goes into detail about Jesus, describing how God Himself was manifested in the flesh, how He appeared in the flesh as a baby born in a manger, how He was justified by the spirit of God. It even says He was seen by angels because He was, in fact, in Heaven and was made by God. Angels are in heaven, so they had to have seen Jesus before God gave Him the command to come down from His rightful place beside His father, be born of a virgin, and die on a cross to save the entire human race from their sins.

It then describes Jesus in even more detail, talking about how He preached among the Gentiles and into many other lands such as Samaria and Jerusalem and told them of the good news of God. He wasn't afraid to admit the truth. He also wasn't afraid to be the truth. Many people all over the world believed in Jesus as the one true God.

He is still believed in by millions of Christians worldwide in the United States and even in many other countries. So many know that He is the one true Messiah and their Savior. They know that He came to save them from the punishment of their sins so that they could have a rightful place beside God in Heaven.

He was then taken up into His eternal glory at Pentecost, on the mountain before his twelve disciples. They were in much shock and awe watching Him go up into Heaven before their very eyes. They knew that He wasn't gone forever and that they would see Him again one day. Although, they didn't know when. The mystery from which true godliness springs is great, in that only Jesus Himself can and will forever be the very definition of true godliness.

No one on Earth can mimic His words, preaching, actions, or His very own divine relationship with His Heavenly Father. It is a good thing that you can't figure out the mystery of godliness because beyond that are all the answers to life. The answers can only be found in God's one true son, Jesus. Remember, sometimes it's a blessing to not know all the answers about life.

Has anyone ever asked you how you know God? What did you tell them? Did you tell them that He saved you from your ways of sin and turned you towards Him?

____

____

____

____

____

____

If someone has ever asked you about who Jesus is, how would you best de-scribe Him in both the true God and true man sense? Did this passage ignite a fire in your heart to tell the world about Jesus?

____

____

____

____

____

Has anyone asked you about who Jesus was and is? How did you approach that topic of discussion? What did you say to that person?

____

____

____

____

____

How did you describe Him as both true God and true man to the person who asked about Him? What is your favorite part of this passage? What is the most surprising part of this passage for you? What did you learn from this passage about Jesus?

____

____

____

____

____

Did this passage remind you to continually let God have all the answers you are looking for in your life and to let Him be the answer to all the questions you may have in life?

____

____

____

WEEK 46

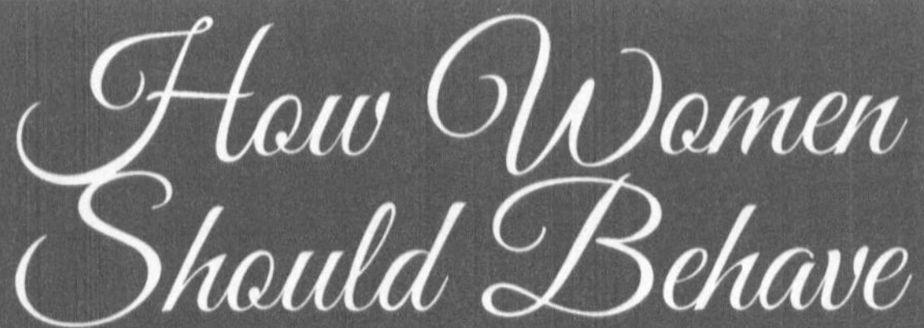

SCRIPTURE READINGS:

Day One: 1 Corinthians 11:3 (The Head of a Wife)

Day Two: 1 Timothy 2:11-15 (Submissive Women)

Day Three: Ephesians 5:22 (Submit to Your Husbands)

Day Four: Colossians 3:18 (Husbands Love Your Wives)

Day Five: 1 Timothy 3: 11 (Be A Dignified Wife)

Day Six: Genesis 1:27 (Created in God's Image)

Day Seven: 1 Timothy 5:14 (Young Widows Can Marry)

"The aged women likewise, that they be in behavior as becometh holiness, not false accusers, not given to much wine, teachers of good things;[4] That they may teach the young women to be sober, to love their husbands, to love their children,[5] To be discreet, chaste, keepers at home, good, obedient to their own husbands, that the word of God be not blasphemed." Titus 2:3-5

The older women can be taught to be reverent in the way they live, so they can teach the younger women how to live their lives in obedience to Christ. To be reverent means to feel and show deep respect for others. The older women can use their knowledge and wisdom to teach the younger women to respect others in their lives, whether it's to their friends, their kids, their bosses, and especially their spouses.

The older women can also teach the younger generation to not drink too much wine and only have wine in moderation. They can teach the younger women in their lives that they can have a glass of wine here and there, but they should teach the younger women to care for their bodies and treat their bodies as the holy temple that God designed them to be. That means not getting drunk, even if it seems like it's the "fun" thing to do. You can tell the younger women of your experiences with alcohol to help younger women understand alcohol's effects on people. You can also teach the younger women to not be slanderous towards other people. Being slanderous means speaking false and malicious statements about people.

You can teach the women around you to not spread mean or false information about other people in their life. You can remind them of the effect that every word can have on people. It can cause you to lose your job, your family, or the friendships that you cherish. Being slanderous can also cause deep trust issues between you and your family, so it's important to keep a guard over your mouth at all times. If you can share any of the things you have learned in your life, you can spare many women in your life a lot of heartaches.

You can also urge the younger women in your life to love their husbands and children with everything they have within them, to always be gentle in their speech and with their words towards their husbands and in front of their kids. Remind them that kids see, hear, and pick up how things are said and done. They learn from their parents' examples.

Remind women that their kids will mimic what they are doing and say to each other, remind them to always make sure that they do everything they can to show Godly, calm behavior in front of their kids. Remind them that being kind is the best option.

DISCUSSION QUESTIONS:

What wisdom can you teach any younger women such as your daughters, sisters, nieces, friends, granddaughters about being Godly examples to others in their lives?

____

____

____

____

____

How can you teach them to love their children and husbands no matter how they may be feeling in any given moment or situation? How can you set a Godly example for them all in your marriage and in your speech and conduct?

____

____

____

____

____

What things have you done to teach them that their words have the power to build up or to destroy people at any time? What is your favorite part of this Bible passage?

____

____

____

____

____

JOURNAL QUESTIONS:

What did you learn from this Bible passage? What part of the passage is sometimes hard for you to keep in practice?

____

____

____

____

____

Has anyone older such as your mom, grandma, aunt, great aunt, sister, or your cousin, ever given you the type of advice talked about in this passage?

____

____

____

____

____

What was your reaction to their advice?

____

____

____

____

____

WEEK 47

SCRIPTURE READINGS:

Day One: Romans 5:1-2 (Justified Through God)

Day Two: Jeremiah 33:3 (Call on God)

Day Three: James 2:17-18 (Faith by My Works)

Day Four: Hebrews 11:1-2 (Assurance of Things Hoped For)

Day Five: Romans 10:17 (Hearing the Word of Christ)

Day Six: Mark 9:23 (All Things are Possible)

Day Seven: 1 Corinthians 16:13 (Stand Firm in Faith)

You will go through hard times in your life. There is no avoiding hard times in life. Sometimes things hit you when you least expect it, and you left reeling from the shock and the pain, wondering what just happened. Sometimes God allows you to go through a hard time to strengthen you as a person. He also lets hard times come in your life to strengthen your faith and your belief in Him. Even though it is very hard to understand why things happen, God knows exactly why those difficult things have happened in your life. He hears you when you cry out from the pain of losing someone you love. He sees you crying on your knees when a loved one gets diagnosed with an incurable disease. He knows the pain you're going through when a friend walks out of your life for no reason.

Jesus also wants to help you find the reassurance that you can only have through your faith and hope in Him. This Bible passage says your faith is the substance of the things you hope for and the evidence of things that are not seen. That means that even though you may not find your answers to your questions in the time frame or in the way you'd like, you can cling to the hope you find in Christ.

Your faith is the only thing that has gotten you this far in your life. When you thought you couldn't take another step, be assured that is when God picked you up and carried you the rest of the way until you could stand on your own again. When you thought your emotions were crashing over you and you had no control of them, that is when Christ came over you like a warm blanket and enveloped you with His peace that surpasses all human understanding.

When you felt as though you were no good for anyone or anything and that you didn't have a purpose in your life, that is when God whispers in your ear, "my child, try again. I have you in the palm of my hand. Don't give up. Your story is not done yet.

I have a wonderful plan and a great purpose for your life." Rest in the assurance of the things that you don't see in this lifetime. Even though you don't see God, you can feel His love, peace, and power in your life, no matter what you may be going through.

DISCUSSION QUESTIONS:

How is your faith? Is it shaken, or do you think you have a strong faith?
Have you ever had times in your life where you were shaken to your very
core?

____

____

____

____

____

How did you feel in those moments? Did you fall on your knees and beg
God to spare you from the heartache and ask Him why those things were
happening to you, or did you wallow and lament in your circumstances?

____

____

____

____

____

How did God strengthen your faith even in the middle of your circumstances?

____

____

____

____

____

JOURNAL QUESTIONS:

What has life thrown at you that made you lose faith? What have you done to reclaim the victory that you have in Christ?

____

____

____

____

____

Do you believe that your faith has seen you through every moment, even up to this point? Do you believe that you will see the assurance of things that are unseen here on Earth once you get to Heaven?

____

____

____

____

____

Do you have the assurance of the unseen things? Where in your life do you need to have the hope and assurance of the things you don't see yet? What things are you waiting to be revealed by God in your faith journey?

____

____

____

____

WEEK 48

SCRIPTURE READINGS:

Day One: James 3:17 (Wisdom from Above)

Day Two: Proverbs 3:13-18 (Blessed with Wisdom)

Day Three: Proverbs 1:7 (Beginning of Knowledge)

Day Four: Ephesians 5:15-17 (Be Careful Where You Walk)

Day Five: Proverbs 19:20 (Accept Instruction)

Day Six: Proverbs 12:15 (Accept Advice)

Day Seven: Proverbs 10:23 (Wisdom Is Pleasure)

"If any of you lack wisdom, let him ask of God, that giveth to all men liberally, and upbraideth not; and it shall be given him." James 1:5

Have you ever cried out for wisdom in your life? You're not the only one. So often, women think they can take care of everything that life throws at them. Then life kind of slaps them in the face and makes them realize they don't know how to handle everything. It's completely okay to not understand everything in life. It's ok to have moments of anger at your kids, as long as you realize that you were wrong for yelling at them, apologize and mean it with your full heart. It's ok to have arguments with your husband, as long as you realize that almost every argument is a silly one. If something needs to be addressed, only talk about it with each other when you're both in the right frame of mind and can discuss things calmly.

It's ok to wonder why things didn't work out in your life with a relationship or with a friendship. You may never know why things went south the way they did, but in your heart, you'll eventually begin to understand that God was only protecting you from more pain. It's ok to have moments where you don't know what to say or do. It's ok to break down and cry.

Do something that takes your mind off the pain, whether it's taking a hot bath, drinking a favorite drink from Starbucks, or eating out by yourself. It's ok to ask God questions. He wants you to ask big questions. He also wants you to remember that the pain you're in right now is not your final destination. You won't be in this position forever. Don't stay wallowing in your pain for too long because it can and will destroy you if you let it.

God's word says if you lack wisdom, you can ask Him for wisdom to get through your certain situation. He gives to you generously without finding fault in you for even asking the questions or for sinning. He doesn't see you as a burden for asking questions about your life. He wants to help you become wise no matter what you're going through in your life.

If you ask for wisdom, it will be given to you. Be careful what you ask for, though, because some answers that you ask for may not be what you wanted to hear. But no matter what guidance and answers you get from God, believe that He is telling you those things to strengthen your faith and make you a wiser person.

In what areas of your life do you lack wisdom? Have you approached God and asked Him for wisdom and guidance in your life? Where are you in your wondering and your questions?

____

____

____

____

____

Have you ever been afraid or uncertain to ask God for wisdom? How has God helped you understand certain situations?

____

____

____

____

____

What has God revealed to you in those moments of severe pain? What has God revealed to you in your darkest moments of wondering things about your life? What kind of wisdom has been given to you in your deepest moments of soul searching?

____

____

____

____

____

JOURNAL QUESTIONS:

What has God taught you about asking for wisdom? What surprises you about this bible passage?

____

____

____

____

____

Are you surprised that you can come to God and ask Him for wisdom no matter what you're going through? What have you learned about yourself and what you can and can't handle?

____

____

____

____

What kind of wisdom have you gained throughout your life? What kind of wisdom are you praying, hoping, and believing that you will get? Do you believe that you will receive the wisdom that you ask for?

____

____

____

____

WEEK 49

SCRIPTURE READINGS:

Day One: Romans 12:2 (Transform Your Mind)

Day Two: Galatians 1:10 (Who Are You Living For?)

Day Three: Mathew 22:37 (Love God with All Your Heart...)

Day Four: Mathew 6:33 (Seek God's Kingdom First)

Day Five: 2 Corinthians 5:17 (New Creation in Christ)

Day Six: Romans 14:8 (Live and Die to Christ)

Day Seven: Mathew 6:24 (Can't Serve Two Masters)

"Forasmuch then as Christ hath suffered for us in the flesh, arm yourselves likewise with the same mind: for he that hath suffered in the flesh hath ceased from sin; ² That he no longer should live the rest of his time in the flesh to the lusts of men, but to the will of God." 1 Peter 4:1-2

Christ suffered the most brutal and painful death in the history of all deaths. He was whipped, beaten, nailed to a cross by his wrists and feet, and left to suffocate to death. He died on the cross to save all of humanity from eternal punishment in hell. That's the ultimate sacrifice. No one else in history has ever made that type of sacrifice for his friends, family, or for all the people on earth. He loved you so much that He willingly went to the cross and took the punishment that you deserve.

This Bible passage points you in the right direction and tells you that since Christ suffered in His body, you too should do the same thing and arm yourself with the same attitude, the same love, the same giving spirit, the same selflessness that Jesus exhibited on the cross. It says whoever suffers in the body is done with sin. Jesus was holy His entire life. He didn't make a mistake, and He didn't sin in His entire life.

If you're living your life in obedience to Christ, it doesn't mean that you won't sin as Jesus never sinned, but it does mean that you're trying to live your best life to be an example of Jesus. You will sin and fail every day of your life, but God knew that you would sin. As long as He sees you trying to learn how to behave and sees you trying to not do that same sin repeatedly, He is proud of you. If you try your best to not live in sin, that's all He asks. If you ask for forgiveness for each and every sin you commit on any given day, you're trying to live by Him. You're trying to rid yourself of the sin and live for God's will.

If you're suffering with the same mindset that Christ suffered on the cross, you have the right attitude. You're willingly suffering for yourself, your friends, your family, and anyone else you know. You are willing to go to the ends of the earth for the ones you love and even willing to risk your life for those you don't know. You're willing to do anything to teach the world about the goodness of God even if you get hurt, ridiculed, mocked, and even if you're rejected by people for proclaiming the good news of Christ and what He has done for you. It even means that you're willing to die trying to tell others about Christ.

DISCUSSION QUESTIONS:

How are you living in obedience to Christ? How are you suffering with
Christ? What has God taught you through your suffering?

____

____

____

____

Where have you gone wrong in your life and given in to sin? How do you
get past the feeling of wanting to live for sin and instead actually turn yourself and your life around and live in obedience to God?

____

____

____

____

How has He helped you turn your life around and helped you live for Him?

____

____

____

____

JOURNAL QUESTIONS:

What things have you done to keep your eyes on God instead of on the things of this world?

____

____

____

____

____

How can you train your mind, body, and soul to want to live in obedience to Christ? How can you let go of your sin and cling to the promises that God gives you as long as you walk in obedience to Him?

____

____

____

____

____

What has God revealed to you when you walk in obedience?

____

____

____

____

____

WEEK 50
Knowledge About Faith

SCRIPTURE READINGS:

Day One: Colossians 3:16 (Enjoy Wisdom)

Day Two: Proverbs 17:27-28 (Have Ears of The Wise)

Day Three: Luke 21:15 (God Gives You A Mouth for Wisdom)

Day Four: Proverbs 3:7 (Don't Be Wise in Your Own Eyes)

Day Five: 1 Corinthians 1:30 (Wisdom from Jesus)

Day Six: Ecclesiastes 8:1 (No One Is Wise)

Day Seven: Proverbs 11:2 (Humble with Wisdom)

"And beside this, giving all diligence, add to your faith virtue; and to virtue knowledge;⁶ And to knowledge temperance; and to temperance patience; and to patience godliness; ⁷ And to godliness brotherly kindness; and to brotherly kindness charity. ⁸ For if these things be in you, and abound, they make you that ye shall neither be barren nor unfruitful in the knowledge of our Lord Jesus Christ."
2 Peter 1:5-8

In everything that you do, make sure to add godliness to your faith. Strengthen your faith by exercising it every day. Read daily devotionals and read Bible verses every day. Spend time with other believers and pray for your brothers and sisters in Christ, and ask them to do the same thing for you. Add knowledge to your faith by discovering more about God and more about your own character and your own life every day. Learn something new every day, and learn to enjoy every day, no matter what may be happening. If you can learn something new every day, you will teach yourself new and exciting things.

To your knowledge, you can add self-control by keeping calm in the middle of stressful and uncertain situations. If you learn to keep calm no matter what is happening inside you or around you, you will think more rationally and clearly. You will then be able to complete tasks quicker and with more efficiency.

Think about the last time you were worked up over a task not being easy to do. You probably allowed yourself to vent and be upset about it instead of taking a deep breath, then saying, "Lord, please help me be able to stay calm as I complete this difficult task. Help me to be able to think clearly and rationally." Once you start exhibiting self-control, you can practice your perseverance in those situations. Whenever tasks get tough, pray for God to give you wisdom and strength to understand the task in front of you.

From there, you can add godliness to everything you do and speak. Just do your best to act the way Jesus did in His daily life. When you screw up, ask God and anyone that you hurt for forgiveness. Then you can add mutual affection and love to everyone in your life. Even though it will be tough to show mutual affection and to love certain people, God knows that you're not perfect, and He isn't expecting you to be perfect. All He wants you to do is try your best.

If you try your best, that is all God can ask of you. You're living by His example as often as you can. If you get and keep these qualities of God every day, you will be very productive and knowledgeable about the Lord. With your knowledge, you can teach others about what it takes to know Christ, how He changed your life, and how He helps you persevere through trials in life.

What tasks do you struggle with within your daily life? What knowledge have you asked God to give to you? How can you practice godliness in your life?

____

____

____

____

____

Where do you need to practice godliness, mutual affection, and love in your life, at your job, at home, or at school?

____

____

____

____

____

What has God taught you about perseverance in your faith walk? What do you hope to know about God in your life? What have you learned about God so far in your faith walk?

____

____

____

____

____

Have you practiced all of these things mentioned in the Bible passage? What is your favorite part of this passage?

____

____

____

____

____

Where can you start having discipline in your faith walk each day, so you can become even more knowledgeable about how to walk by faith and act the way Jesus acts in every situation?

____

____

____

____

____

WEEK 51

Be Merciful to The Doubters

SCRIPTURE READINGS:

Day One: James 1:6 (Ask for Faith)

Day Two: Mathew 21:21 (Don't Doubt)

Day Three: Mathew 14:21 (Why Did You Doubt?)

Day Four: Luke 24:38 (Why Do Doubts Arise?)

Day Five: John 20:27 (Don't Doubt, But Believe)

Day Six: Romans 14:23 (Whoever Doubts Is Condemned)

Day Seven: Mark 11:22-25 (Keep the Faith)

²⁰"But ye, beloved, building up yourselves on your most holy faith, praying in the Holy Ghost. ²¹ Keep yourselves in the love of God, looking for the mercy of our Lord Jesus Christ unto eternal life. ²² And of some have compassion, making a difference: ²³ And others save with fear, pulling them out of the fire; hating even the garment spotted by the flesh." Jude 1:20-23

Build yourselves up by exercising your faith every day. Take the time to pray every day, whether it's in the morning, afternoon, in the evening, or as you fall asleep. Keep as close to God as you possibly can in everything you do in your life. Keep yourself in God's love as you wait for Jesus' return and as you wait to be taken to Heaven for all eternity. Do everything that you can to be in tune with your faith. Go to church and be in fellowship with other believers. Look for God's mercy and show the same mercy He shows to you every day of your life. Have compassion for everyone you encounter because everyone is going through a battle that you know nothing about. If someone is going through a hard time, take time to pray for them.

Be merciful to anyone who doubts the goodness of the Lord instead of casting judgment, saying, "this person doesn't know what they're missing. They really don't know about God." Instead, you can tell them all about salvation and how it has changed your life for the better and how it can change your life for the better too. If they ask you questions, you can tell them the story of how you found Jesus and how His love and mercy have impacted your life.

You can actually play a valuable part in saving someone from the eternal fire of hell by sharing the good news of salvation with them. It is amazing to know that you can be a part of someone accepting Jesus Christ as their Savior.

If there are people who don't accept the things you say about Christ, be merciful to those who doubt the goodness of Jesus Christ and the salvation He offers to them freely. You can still talk to them with a guard over your heart and a guard over your mouth. You can choose carefully what you say to those doubters. (There will be plenty of people who don't want to hear about Him and think that He is fake).

This passage even warns you to tell them about God but to show mercy to those doubters and to have a bit of fear about telling them about Christ, so you're prepared to get away from them if they keep rejecting the good news. It also warns you that you can hate the clothes they wear if they're still corrupted by this world's views and chose not to believe in God.

DISCUSSION QUESTIONS:

Have you ever encountered anyone who thought Jesus wasn't real or that salvation wasn't real? What did you do in response to their thoughts?

____

____

____

____

____

What have you done to keep your faith strong every day? How have you shown mercy to the people who ask you about God but doubt His goodness?

____

____

____

____

____

Have you ever brought another person to find salvation in Jesus Christ? How did you feel knowing that you played a part in saving their life?

____

____

____

____

____

What is the most challenging part of being a merciful Christian to the doubters?

____

____

____

____

____

What is your favorite thing to say to someone who asks about God? Have you ever played a part in helping a stranger or a friend find salvation?

____

____

____

____

____

What was the most challenging part of talking to that person? Did it feel good to have a part in saving someone's life through the good news of Jesus?

____

____

____

____

____

WEEK 52

Second Coming of Jesus

SCRIPTURE READINGS:

Day One: 1 Thessalonians 4:16-17 (Trumpet Sounds)

Day Two: Hebrews 9:28 (Eagerly Wait for God)

Day Three: Revelation 1:7 (Coming on The Clouds)

Day Four: 2 Peter 3:10 (The Lord Comes Like A Thief)

Day Five: Mathew 24:36 (No One Knows the Hour)

Day Six: Mathew 24:44 (Be Ready for Jesus)

Day Seven: Revelations 22:12 (He Is Coming Soon)

[12] "And, behold, I come quickly; and my reward is with me, to give every man according as his work shall be.[13] I am Alpha and Omega, the beginning and the end, the first and the last... [18]For I testify unto every man that heareth the words of the prophecy of this book, If any man shall add unto these things, God shall add unto him the plagues that are written in this book:[19] And if any man shall take away from the words of the book of this prophecy, God shall take away his part out of the book of life, and out of the holy city, and from the things which are written in this book." Revelation 22:12-13, 18-19

Jesus Christ is coming quickly. Always be ready for the time that He comes back. It could be when you least expect Him to return. He carries His reward of salvation with Him to everyone who believes in Him. He will give to each person according to what he has done. So always make sure to behave nicely in your life, no matter who you may be interacting with. If you act angry and irrationally, God sees that and doesn't like that kind of behavior. When He sees you acting nicely to everyone that you come across, whether it's your children, your husband, your boss, or your coworkers, God will reward you for that type of behavior.

It is written that He is the Alpha and Omega, the beginning and the end. He was the first person in Heaven and the first person to create everything on Earth, from the planets to the stars to the sand on the beach and the ocean, to Adam and Eve in the Garden of Eden. He was and is the first and the last. God warns everyone to hear the words of the Lord's prophecy. If anyone adds to the words spoken in the prophecy or adds to what is written in the scroll, God will allow hardships to come upon that person's life.

If anyone takes words away from the scroll or takes any words away from the Lord's prophecy, God will take away that person's place in the Tree of Knowledge of Good and Evil and in the Holy City. The Holy City is Heaven, and "the share in the Tree of Knowledge of Good and Evil" is a person's salvation in Jesus. Let these words be warnings to everyone: Do not add to or take away from the prophecies of God; otherwise, your life will be full of difficulty and strife. Not only that, if you take away or add anything to the prophecies mentioned in the Bible, you will lose your salvation and your place in eternity in Heaven with Jesus.

So, if you want to secure your place in Heaven and your salvation in Jesus, do your best to never take away or add to His divine prophecy. Tell others that add or take away words from His divine prophecy to stop what they are doing, and explain to them gently and sincerely that they need to repent of their sins. If you don't want people in your life to suffer eternal punishment in hell, you can help them see the errors of their ways before it's too late.

DISCUSSION QUESTIONS:

Have you ever added to or taken words out of the Lord's prophecy? Are you shocked by the things mentioned in this passage?

What did this passage teach you about Jesus' second coming? What areas of your life do you need to change before Jesus' second coming?

Have you or anyone you know ever taken away or added to the Lord's prophecy about His second coming?

____

____

____

____

____

Does this passage change the way you view salvation? Do you take your salvation and the salvation of other people in your life that much more seriously after reading this passage?

____

____

____

____

____

www.ingramcontent.com/pod-product-compliance
Lightning Source LLC
Chambersburg PA
CBHW021433150726

47989CB00001B/236